"J.R. Briggs goes beyond giving us a robust theology of failure; he opens his veins and shares his life. He calls us to be faithful not efficient, to live vulnerably without shame. He gives us grace-filled opportunities to be our true selves. If you are a pastor, you need this book!"

JR Woodward, national director of church planting for V3, author of *Creating a Missional Culture*

"If you are struggling in ministry, this book will be like sitting down with a good friend who knows and understands what you are enduring. No quick fixes. No pat answers. No formulas. No judgment. Just gentle wisdom laced with grace to help you continue in God's calling."

Ruth Graham, author of *In Every Pew Sits a Broken Heart*

"*Fail* is like a barn for a tired, overburdened mule. That mule is us: preachers, pastors, leaders in the church. The wonderful gift we are given here is a re-yoking, where we come into that barn and have our yokes removed—which are of impossible weight to carry and manage—and slip into the yoke of Jesus, who carries all the burden of ministry and lets us join him, side by side, on the journey."

Lance Ford, author of *UnLeader* and *The Missional Quest*

"With *Fail*, J.R. Briggs has captured a truth we all crave but fear to articulate. There is not merely grace for the burning- or burnt-out, there is the very life of Christ: full of honesty, meaning and sharp joy. Beyond platitudes or Twitter-quote pep talks, J.R. offers peace, real encouragement, and a better definition of success for Christian ministry. This is the next best thing to sharing the body and blood with people who understand. Failures large and small, visible and invisible, will stand up and shout for J.R.'s wisdom, wit and honesty. I know that I do."

Paul Pastor, associate editor of Christianity Today's *Leadership Journal* and PARSE

"This book is CPR. *Fail* has given me breath for years to come. Within, Briggs offers an engaging, appealing and learned description of the *failed* life, invoking his readers to see afresh the breathtaking journey of all the landmarks along the way. Briggs reminds us that half of resurrection is death. And that, to truly live, we *must* fail. Jesus breathed his Spirit over a group of failed disciples from his cross. That same kind of thing seems to be going on in this book."

A. J. Swoboda, PhD, professor, pastor and author of *Messy*

"God is allowing thousands of men and women to fail. Isn't that wonderful? It is if you can see it from God's perspective. I believe that God, although hurting with you through your pain and loss, is also delighted in your failure. Why? Because he wants so much more for you! J.R. Briggs will give you language for what you're going through, help you find healing where you are and provide you with some handles for the journey ahead. As a man who has experienced his share of failure, I am so glad someone finally had the courage *and* hopefulness to write a book like this one. You'll be glad, too!"

Kevin Colón, neighborhood lead pastor at LifeBridge Christian Church, missional-incarnational coach and consultant at Missio

"J.R. Briggs captures the struggle of pastors in his new book *Fail*. The fear of failure is enough to freeze us in our path to ministry. J.R. not only shows the facts as to how this is affecting ministers across every denomination but also points toward solutions for pastors to find their way out in the midst of failure. Pastors often find themselves incapable, inadequate and even incompetent in the task that God has placed before them. J.R. reminds them that the only hope they have to complete the mission God has placed on their calling is to rely on the Holy Spirit."

Maurice Graham, executive director, Shepherd's Staff Ministry

"Fear of failure is a power that holds many church leaders in a death grip. In this important book, J.R. Briggs boldly speaks from his own experience and that of others, reminding us that failure is inevitable, but the crucial question is how we find grace and eventually recovery in the aftermath of failure. The gospel that we encounter in *Fail* is undoubtedly good news, true liberation for our fearful, weary and broken selves. May we heed its call!"

C. Christopher Smith, coauthor of *Slow Church* and founding editor of *The Englewood Review of Books*

"J.R. Briggs offers a sobering look at the pain, loneliness and shame we pastors regularly face. Like the apostle Paul, he understands that the best ministry happens when we allow it to flow through our own weakness and failure. Reading this book was like 'a kiss from God on my bruises.'"

Aaron Graham, lead pastor, The District Church, Washington, D.C.

"J.R. Briggs has something to say to pastors about our American obsession with 'success.' He holds to the Jesus-endorsed notion that those in ministry are called to faithfulness, not success, and that sometimes faithfulness takes the peculiar form of failure. *Fail* dares to tell the truth and will bring much-needed clarity and comfort to a multitude of ministers who, though faithful, have drunk from the bitter cup of failure."

Brian Zahnd, pastor, Word of Life Church, St. Joseph, Missouri, and author of *A Farewell to Mars*

FAIL

Finding HOPE and GRACE in the Midst of MINISTRY Failure

J.R. Briggs

Foreword by Eugene H. Peterson

IVP Books

An imprint of InterVarsity Press
Downers Grove, Illinois

InterVarsity Press
P.O. Box 1400, Downers Grove, IL 60515-1426
www.ivpress.com
email@ivpress.com

InterVarsity Press® is the book-publishing division of InterVarsity Christian Fellowship/USA®, a movement of students and faculty active on campus at hundreds of universities, colleges and schools of nursing in the United States of America, and a member movement of the International Fellowship of Evangelical Students. For information about local and regional activities, write Public Relations Dept., InterVarsity Christian Fellowship/USA, 6400 Schroeder Rd., P.O. Box 7895, Madison, WI 53707-7895, or visit the IVCF website at www.intervarsity.org.

All Scripture quotations, unless otherwise indicated, are taken from THE HOLY BIBLE, NEW INTERNATIONAL VERSION®, NIV® Copyright © 1973, 1978, 1984, 2011 by Biblica, Inc.™ Used by permission. All rights reserved worldwide.

While all stories in this book are true, some names and identifying information in this book have been changed to protect the privacy of the individuals involved.

Material in chapters 8 and 9 from Dr. Stephen Burrell is used with permission.

Published in association with the literary agency of Wolgemuth & Associates.

Cover design: Cindy Kiple
Interior design: Beth Hagenberg
Images: broken lamp: ©Milk Mike/iStockphoto
broken light bulb: ©imageStock/iStockphoto
shattered light bulb: ©Gudella/iStockphoto

ISBN 978-0-8308-4111-0 (print)
ISBN 978-0-8308-7968-7 (digital)

Printed in the United States of America ∞

Library of Congress Cataloging-in-Publication Data

Briggs, J. R., 1979-
Fail : finding hope and grace in the midst of ministry failure / J.R. Briggs.
pages cm
Includes bibliographical references.
ISBN 978-0-8308-4111-0 (pbk. : alk. paper)
1. Failure (Psychology)—Religious aspects—Christianity. 2. Pastoral theology. I. Title.
BT730.5.B73 2014
253'.2—dc23
2014011880

P	18	17	16	15	14	13	12	11	10	9	8	7	6	5	4	3	2	1
Y	29	28	27	26	25	24	23	22	21	20	19	18	17	16	15	14		

For Jason Sheffield

CONTENTS

FOREWORD

IF THERE IS ONE PIECE OF COUNSEL FOR PASTORS that towers over all else in this book it is this: Failure is not the last word in a pastor's life. But you can't deal with it by yourself. The pastoral vocation is fraught with danger. The kingdom of God is under constant attack. Anyone in the thick of the action (which the pastor certainly is) needs a discerning friend. You can't do this by yourself.

The precipitating event that resulted in the writing of this book was an unexpected and devastating failure. In the process of picking up the pieces of his failure, J.R. Briggs, a young pastor with promising credentials, became aware of just how widespread pastoral failures are in North America. As he looked around him and looked into what others were seeing, he became aware of the dimensions of pastoral failure, grimly underlined by the statistic that fifteen hundred pastors abandon their pastoral vocation every month because of either burnout or contention in their congregations. In the process of surveying the wreckage, licking his own wounds and listening to pastors tell their stories, he realized that the work of being a pastor is, by its very nature, fertile ground for the weeds of failure. But there is also a corollary: failure can serve as compost for enriching the pastoral vocation so that it brings forth thirtyfold and maybe even a hundredfold.

The stories and insights assembled and crafted in this book will go a long way in deconstructing what J.R. Briggs names the "golden calf culture of success," probably the leading contributor to failure among North American church pastors. But he does far more than expose the blasphemy and silliness of the golden calf. Detail by detail he develops in us a pastoral imagination congruent with Jesus—unpretentious, sacrificial, modest, prayerful, obedient, present and bold. All of us who embrace the pastoral vocation need all the help we can get to discern and practice these essential qualities if we are to maintain the purity and focus of our pastoral identity.

While reading *Fail* I recalled the person used by God in my early years of becoming a pastor to rescue me from being seduced by the culture of the golden calf. It was fifty-five years ago. My rescuer was a priest, and I never did get to know his name.

I was new at this pastor business, with minimal experience— three years as an associate pastor at a large city church and recently assigned by my denomination to be the organizing pastor of a new congregation. The location was a small town, fast becoming a suburb of Baltimore. First Presbyterian Church, located in the center of the town, was landlocked, with minimal parking and no room to expand. They requested the denomination for help in organizing a sister congregation. I was given the job.

This was the 1960s, the decade of the "death of God." Church attendance was diminishing all over the country. Starting new churches was one of the primary strategies for recovering momentum. Much was being written and many techniques suggested for providing a transfusion of evangelistic energy into a failing church. Anxiety, some of it verging on hysteria, pervaded the church's leadership.

Those of us who had been assigned to develop new congregations felt the pressure to succeed. There was a lot at stake. And there was no lack of experts on the sidelines telling us precisely what to do to stanch the flow of blood and get the church back on its feet again.

Previous to this, my favorite text describing church, a text preached by every pastor who showed up in our small town, was "You are beautiful as Tirzah, my love, comely as Jerusalem, terrible as an army with banners" (Song 6:4). But in my present circumstances, the air filled with statistical gloom and desperate attempts to repackage our image to appeal to the secularized expectations of a "generation that knew not Joseph," the eroticized, lissome Tirzah and the terrible-as-an-army-with-banners had been scrapped and replaced with fresh imagery provided by American business. When I wasn't looking, my vocation as pastor was being relentlessly diminished and corrupted.

This was the Americanization of the congregation. Each congregation was turned into a market for religious consumers, an ecclesiastical business run along the lines of advertising techniques and organizational flow charts, and then energized by impressive motivational "vision statements."

For about a year I had been attempting to internalize and understand the direction of the leaders in "congregational renewal" who, in their writings and seminars, were orienting me in my new work of organizing a congregation. I had booked a flight to Los Angeles to attend one of these seminars. Luckily I had forgotten to pack the latest must-read book by one of the accredited gurus. I saw a book title in the airport bookstore that caught my eye, and I bought *The Diary of a Country Priest* to stand in as a substitute for my assigned guru. I had never heard of the author, Georges Bernanos. I bought it simply on the strength of the title.

I was a new pastor in my first congregation. The priest writing this diary was also in his first appointment. We were the same age, thirty years. I anticipated finding a companion in what for both of us was new territory as novices in a complex vocation. We had a lot to learn. There were, of course, considerable differences. He was French and a Catholic priest; I was an American and a Protestant pastor. He lived in a country village in celibacy on the edge of poverty; I lived in a fairly affluent suburb with a wife and new daughter. His parish was centuries old with a proper chapel in which to worship; my congregation, such as it was, worshiped in the basement of my home.

I assumed I was reading the actual diary of an actual priest. Something about the *Diary* caught my imagination almost immediately. The simplicity of this priest's life, the care he took to understand and care for his parishioners, the deep loneliness he endured, the incomprehension with which he was treated by the established priests in his presbytery, the daunting task that I had entered into of forming a congregation out of these thirty to forty misfits in my neighborhood, my own fear of not fitting in and failing.

Upon arriving in Los Angeles eight hours later, I knew I had made a fast friend.

On the return trip to Baltimore three days later I reread the *Diary*. I continued to be gripped by the story. The discernments involved in following Jesus, worked out in conditions of poverty and humiliation, struck me with a depth of authenticity and gospel obedience that I hardly imagined possible.

I later learned that the book was a novel. I read it again. Fiction though it is, there is not a false note in it—every sentence rings true. Through numerous rereadings it has permeated my imagination and has become a major defense against the golden calf. For me it is a major witness to the nuances and subtleties involved in following the actual, revealed Jesus in a culture that has installed religious conventions and fantasies in place of the real thing.

The words the country priest wrote in his diary as he was dying strike most readers as accurate: "Grace is everywhere." The stories told by Georges Bernanos in *Diary of a Country Priest* and by J.R. Briggs in *Fail* are stories that place experienced failure in a redemptive and hopeful context, in an extensive *biblical* and local *community* context. Once we get started, our imaginations, at least mine, keep adding stories: what David experienced in the betrayals of first Ahithophel (Ps 55), then Absalom (Ps 3) and later Mephibosheth; what Jesus experienced in the denials of Peter and the betrayal of Judas. Accounts of misunderstanding and betrayal and failure, whether perceived or actual, are threaded through the fabric of kingdom living—which makes the counsel of these witnesses, whether fictional or actual, life giving. *Fail* is not the last word. "Grace is everywhere" is the last word.

Eugene H. Peterson
Professor Emeritus of Spiritual Theology
Regent College, Vancouver

INTRODUCTION

THE F-Word

But he said to me, "My grace is sufficient for you,
for my power is made perfect in weakness."
Therefore I will boast all the more gladly
about my weaknesses, so that Christ's
power may rest on me.

2 Corinthians 12:9

The spiritual journey is not a career or success story.
It is a series of humiliations of the false self that
becomes more and more profound.

Thomas Keating, *The Human Condition*

I AM HOPEFUL AND DISILLUSIONED about the future of the church.
I've asked dozens of pastors and church leaders to describe the
lowest point in their ministry. Too often the answer is "Right

now." A few have even said rhetorically, "When has it not been a low point?" As I survey the landscape of churches, I see an overwhelming amount of lonely, wounded and discouraged pastors whose souls seem to be on life support. The thought jolts me, *Is this what Jesus had in mind for pastors—a life absent of joy and peace, and with omnipresent stress and emotional hardship?*

A few years ago I was deeply frustrated about being a pastor. More specifically, I was discouraged by the assumed requirements of becoming a "successful" pastor. In the midst of the frustration I had an idea. It was counterintuitive—and slightly satirical—but I could not shake it. After a few days of reflection, I opened my laptop, wrote out my thoughts and posted it on my blog:

> I've been to my fair share of church conferences in the past decade. Some have been helpful. Most have not.
>
> The process is similar at just about every conference: thousands of dollars are put into marketing budgets, glossy fliers and paying significant honoraria to the top Christian leaders in the country—recognized by the size of their congregation's weekend attendance—to come and share how their church got to be so large, innovative and attractive. The programming at these conferences is flawless and the presentations are perfect—but for attendees, the drive home is crappy.
>
> I'm a big supporter of learning from wise women and men who have led their congregations well. But it seems the vast majority of pastors who've attended these conferences walk away feeling guilty, insecure or like utter failures. Attendees can often feel like they can't possibly relate to the speakers on the platform. It can breed insecurity and comparison.

Or, maybe worse, we walk away thinking we've found the silver bullet, the key concept or the perfect model that we can take back home and implement on Sunday. We've been convinced the key method/approach/model/style will solve the problem of why our church isn't doubling in attendance every three and a half months. Sometimes conferences for pastors and church leaders slowly and persuasively convince me that I—we—are the head of our church. Last I checked, Jesus is still the head of it.

What if there was an Epic Fail Pastors Conference (with the tag line of the event: "Where leaders put their worst foot forward")? I'm convinced the church needs something like this.

Within a few hours of its posting, my phone began ringing and my email inbox began to fill at a significant rate. Within just a few weeks I had received thousands of blog hits and hundreds of emails, phone calls and text messages from pastors and church leaders across North America, each speaking with a sense of urgency about the dire need for a conference like I had suggested. I was astounded by the response. In almost a decade of posting hundreds of thoughts on my blog, nothing I had written had received this level of attention.

I had unintentionally touched a nerve. Pastors need safe and intentional spaces in which to talk about their failures, identity and mistakes. Yet there is little opportunity. Numerous individuals made commitments to do whatever it took to turn this idea into a reality. A few friends and I began to dream about whether this idea might actually be a worthy pursuit. Did we have enough courage to host an event like this, something completely counterintuitive from other ministry conferences? And if we did, would anyone show up to an event on failure?

Hosting a Conference on Failure

Inevitably, we decided to pull the trigger. I formed a team to help create an authentic and honest space for pastors to discuss what most had thought about but few were actually talking about. We wanted to give much-needed space to process our own stories of failure and see how the waters of the gospel cut through the canyons of our brokenness.

We hosted the first Epic Fail Pastors Conference in my community of Lansdale, Pennsylvania, a small suburb on the north side of Philadelphia. No glossy fliers. No big marketing budget. We called our presenters "Experts on Failure." In order to keep costs low we couldn't pay our speakers. No large arena with stadium seating. Instead, we rented an old, locals-only, hole-in-the-wall bar where the beer is cheap and the food is even cheaper. We were told the building was originally a church, but years ago it failed. The building was later sold to an Elks Lodge, who then sold it to a local businessman who turned it into a bar. Pool tables replaced pews. Beer signs replaced stained-glass windows. Profanity-laced rap songs at a teeth-rattling volume replaced soothing hymns accompanied by an organ. Considering the nature of the event, the location seemed perfect.

We wanted pastors and former pastors to tell stories, reflect, pray, listen, eat meals slowly, connect with others and take Communion together. The goal was not to celebrate success, yet we were not looking to celebrate failure either. Our goal was simply to celebrate faithfulness in ministry (regardless of the outcome), to highlight our need for grace and to acknowledge Jesus as the foundation of all we do in ministry and in life.

We anticipated a raw but hope-filled event—and it was. A friend encouraged me to keep this passage from 2 Corinthians 4 as the foundation of our time:

But we have this treasure in jars of clay to show that this all-surpassing power is from God and not from us. We are hard pressed on every side, but not crushed; perplexed, but not in despair; persecuted, but not abandoned; struck down, but not destroyed. We always carry around in our body the death of Jesus, so that the life of Jesus may also be revealed in our body. For we who are alive are always being given over to death for Jesus' sake, so that his life may also be revealed in our mortal body. So then, death is at work in us, but life is at work in you. (vv. 7-12)

A few verses later:

Therefore we do not lose heart. Though outwardly we are wasting away, yet inwardly we are being renewed day by day. For our light and momentary troubles are achieving for us an eternal glory that far outweighs them all. So we fix our eyes not on what is seen, but on what is unseen, since what is seen is temporary, but what is unseen is eternal. (vv. 16-18)

Deep in my bones I was convinced many pastors wrestle with thoughts of failure—and yet few are willing and able to talk about it. We knew it would be a risk to host an event to help pastors develop a robust theology of failure, but we sensed it was worth the risk of failure to do so.

Looking back, it is easy to remember the maddening process of trying to plan a conference on failure. It is filled with second-guessing, incessant questioning of one's own motives and seemingly endless Catch-22 situations. What if we plan this conference on failure and four people sign up? Did we succeed because we failed at an epic failure conference? Or what if ten thousand people sign up? Would I be a sellout and a hypocrite by pulling off an extremely successful conference on failure? It was almost enough to make me lose my mind. Can you imagine the headline: "Epic Fail Pastors Conference Canceled Due to Low Registration"? Could we recover from such irony? A first-time, low-budget conference on failure held in a failed-church-turned-bar in a suburb of Philadelphia that is anything but a tourist destination seemed like a large enough risk.

We had originally thought that it would be a small, regional event. We were surprised that people traveled from seventeen states—some not knowing many of the details, but knowing deep down they had to attend.

During the final session of the conference, a pastor named Collin raised his hand and said, "Thanks so much for providing a space like this. It was totally worth the time, energy and effort to be here. I hope you do it again. If you do, I'll be back." The statement was affirming. But what made the statement significant is that Collin lives in Australia. I asked him why he would travel literally to the other side of the world to talk about failure with pastors. His response was saddening: "I can't find anyone in my province who is willing to talk honestly about failure and ministry. I can't even find anyone on my continent. This was the only space I could find."

Initially, all the buzz and attention was encouraging, and yet it grieved me deeply—clear evidence there is a lack of safe space for pastors. What would inspire someone to fly halfway across the globe to talk about failure? Why would a pastor drive 1,200 miles by himself to spend three days in a bar? Why would a pastor be so afraid to address failure he felt he had to tell his elders his was going "on vacation" as cover for attending, believing his elders would be upset?

I realized there should be dozens of these types of conferences for pastors across the country. I was not hoping for all the attention.

All I was trying to do was find a place to appropriately process my fear of and experience with failure with other courageous people. Because I could not find such a space, we sought to create one ourselves. And somehow, to our great relief, people showed up. People shared their stories and struggles with refreshing courage. They opened up about their battles with depression and suicidal thoughts, their terror of failure and their broken hearts over a failed church nine years prior. They shared how dry, lost and alone they felt. I looked at my watch. We were seventeen minutes in and people were standing up telling complete strangers stories of pain, loss, fear and deep wounds. Seventeen minutes. There were no superstars, no impressive videos, no greenrooms and no lanyards. There were no vendors pushing their products, no book tables to purchase conference resources and no announcements from sponsors. All I could think was, *We are on to something here.*

No one left impressed that we put on a stellar performance during the conference. Pastors told us they experienced the undeniable presence of God in the room. This gritty bar had become a sacred space, marked with courageous admissions, powerful times of worship and significant healing.

At the end of the event, pastors wrote down their thoughts on index cards:

- *My resistance to vulnerability is feeding my deepest shame.*

- *Epic Failures make for good Pastors.*

- *Facing and embracing failure is the most successful thing I can do.*

- *The gospel is enough . . .*

- *In my shame, I see God identifying with me.*

- *I'm not giving up on vulnerability.*

The event culminated in a time of sharing Communion. We reveled in its mysterious power: the broken body and spilled blood of Jesus, given so that a broken world could be made whole again. We communed—with God and each other—handing out loaves of bread and glasses of wine. We invited people into extended and unrushed conversations with those around their tables about what God was doing in their journey through their brokenness. "Finish the loaves," we told them. "Bottoms up on the wine. Linger and talk and pray until it's all gone." There was laughter and prayer and tears and refills. It was, as one retired pastor put it, "a kiss from God on our bruises."

Confession. Humility. Healing. Hope. Jesus. It was, by God's grace, a success.

Our team has hosted and facilitated several Epic Fail Pastors events in different places throughout the country—and we continue to do so—each one similar yet beautifully messy and noticeably unique. We continue to hear stories laced with painful pasts, look into the eyes of exhausted leaders, see the sagging shoulders of discouragement and listen to the desperate longings for deep repair. We know there are many other pastors who would benefit from intentional spaces and sacred conversations to process failure outside the context of an Epic Fail Pastors event, which is why I am convinced a book like this needed to be written.

Expectations for a Book on Failure

Why write a book on failure and ministry? Because ministry is fertile ground for failure, and failure is fertile ground for ministry. Other pastors are feeling what you are feeling, wrestling with what you are wrestling with and trying to stumble in the direction of grace. We desperately need a robust theology of failure, something almost entirely absent from the language and psyche of many pastors today. As Paul David Tripp wrote, we must realize the mirrors of ministry success that we are looking into are not accurate and are much more like the curved mirrors at a carnival that distort and mislead us away from who we really are.[1] Breakdowns often lead to breakthroughs—and sometimes failure can be the very thing that provides the breakthrough we need to experience true ministry.

Throughout the book I am going to share stories of wounded pastors. The stories are real, but most of the names have been changed due to the sensitive nature of the topic. I hope you will find a sense of solidarity and connection with these pastors and their stories. My desire is that this book will help you to ruthlessly preach on a daily basis the same gospel to yourself that we so consistently and passionately preach to others. I hope the fullness of grace meets the fullness of truth in your life through the context of failure.

Relatively speaking, our failures and sufferings in North America are minuscule compared to what many of our brothers and sisters around the world experience every day. There are thousands who are persecuted in various oppressive ways because of their trust and faith in Jesus. While our failure and wounds are significant, it is important that we keep them in perspective as we explore this topic in our context.

I refuse to be pithy in my approach to such a significant topic. This will not be filled with moaning and groaning, complaining and sulking. And I hope you do not find a tone of cynicism. (Who wants to spend time reading about that?) Yes, deep pain and severe wounds are real, but I want raw truth and stalwart hope to spill out onto the pages.

This is not a book about how to learn from our failure so we will not fail again. Nor do I offer ways to become even more successful climbing the ministry ladder. You will find no surefire answers or fail-proof methods. The focus is to encourage, support and help those who have experienced—or fear experi-

encing—failure and are in need of a perspective on grace and
the hope of a recovery. At the end of the book I've included
study questions for personal processing or group discussion.
I've also provided additional resources to further your learning
and processing.

In addition, this book will probably disappoint you. In all
likelihood I will fail in writing a book about failure. The topic of
failure and ministry is so vast I cannot possibly cover every topic,
emotion or situation in one book, regardless of its length. Some
failures are on a systemic level; others are on a personal level.
Some failures are tragic and devastating; others are smaller and
less discernible. Some failures are moral; others are merely practical. Plumbing its depths is nearly impossible.

While the systemic nature of the failure of denominations, organizations and leadership within the North American church
will be addressed briefly, the bulk of this book deals with the
personal feelings and effects of failure—whether real, perceived
or claimed—in the lives of pastors and Christian leaders. This is
not to say that the systemic issues of church culture should not
be addressed; assuredly, they have been and will continue to be
confronted. There are writers much more wise and insightful than
I who challenge these systemic failures, but this is not such a book.

My qualification to write on this topic comes from firsthand
experience in ministry failure as well as deep-seated fear of
failing as a pastor. Too often I forget the grace and good news
Jesus offers, which is the very reason I need it daily. It's also the
reason I needed to write a book on this topic.

I will not offer a formula for avoiding or an equation for recovering from ministry failure. What I am after is communicating that failure is the crucible of character formation. While
my primary audience is pastors, the book is intended to also
relate to Christian leaders in a variety of contexts: church, para-

church, nonprofits, Christian institutions, mission organizations and so forth. I give you permission to grieve, reflect or rejoice in whatever appropriate expression it may take. I want to give you tools to work through significant issues in order to come out the other side with restored hope.

As I write, I am not trying to slap a Band-Aid on your wounds or throw a few Bible verses your direction in order to make the pain go away. Wounds are serious. They should be handled tenderly and should not be taken lightly. I will refrain from quick answers and easy solutions. I want to abstain from initiating feelings of guilt and shame for what you have or have not done. I want to avoid communicating a works-based gospel. Instead, I want to provide grace-oriented opportunities to lean into the arms of our Father.

May this book be soothing ointment to your heart and healing salve to your soul.

1

FAILURE

The Trigger of Our Biggest Fears

We are fools for Christ, but you are so wise in Christ! We are weak, but you are strong! You are honored, we are dishonored! To this very hour we go hungry and thirsty, we are in rags, we are brutally treated, we are homeless. We work hard with our own hands. When we are cursed, we bless; when we are persecuted, we endure it; when we are slandered, we answer kindly. We have become the scum of the earth, the garbage of the world— right up to this moment.

1 Corinthians 4:10-13

To the degree you face and name and deal with your failures as a leader, to that same extent you will create an environment conducive to growing and retaining productive and committed relationships in ministry. Sometimes the quickest path up is down, and likewise, the surest success comes through being honest about failure.

Dan Allender, *Leading with a Limp*

My Story

Growing up I attended a well-respected, private Christian high school in a city known for its rich history and academic prestige. I was a three-sport athlete—including an all-state selection in basketball. I was awarded one of three leadership scholarships at a reputable Christian college in the Midwest. Shortly after graduating from college, my wife and I married and moved to Colorado Springs to work for a Christian publishing company. This position allowed me to interact closely with Christian leaders and authors. Fresh out of college, I had access to people and opportunities I never thought I would have.

After a few years I was hired to pastor a group of twentysomethings/young adults at the second largest church in Colorado Springs, the evangelical Vatican. I was cutting my teeth among a growing, vibrant group of young adults, and seeing numerical growth and momentum under my leadership. Additionally, I had written three books before I turned twenty-eight.

A few years later Gary, the senior pastor of a megachurch in the Philadelphia area, introduced himself to me and asked if I might be interested in starting an alternative service geared toward those in a post-Christian context (mostly younger adults), similar to what I was currently doing in Colorado Springs. Gary told me he was going to retire in a few years and was looking to groom a young pastor to replace him. I was surprised and honored, but told him I was uncertain I was interested in such a ministry position. He did not waver and encouraged me to join his staff, promising to build into me and mentor me. My wife, Megan, and I sensed what we believed to be God's direction to leave Colorado and move to Philadelphia to join this almost three-thousand-member church to develop a new alternative ministry from the ground up and be mentored by a respected and experienced pastor.

Though we moved to a place where we knew no one, we quickly encountered the sky-high expectations that were placed on us. It was a difficult transition to the culture of the area, trying hard to stave off feelings of loneliness and attempting to carefully navigate the burden of unarticulated expectations. Concurrent to starting this new ministry, I was asked to preach three or four times in that first year. I had never preached to crowds of almost three thousand people—let alone a room larger than three hundred—but for whatever reason, God's favor was on my teaching and the response from the church was affirming. Due to some severe health issues Gary was experiencing, as well as other organizational factors within the church, I was asked to preach more regularly—often in stretches of two to three Sunday mornings per month. Many saw a trajectory of me eventually becoming the senior pastor. I was seen as the heir apparent (some staff members called me "the Golden Boy," which I resented). Because of the sense of inevitability, I felt immense pressure to succeed. I enjoyed teaching and other additional opportunities, but it was quite unsettling.

One Sunday morning between services I walked back to my office to collect my thoughts before preaching again in a few minutes. A well-meaning couple stopped me in the hallway and gushed about my teaching. With all the sincerity and earnestness they could muster, they told me something I will not soon forget: "We just know that you are going to be the next Andy Stanley." I respect Andy Stanley greatly. I am grateful for his ministry. But I was stunned. *Is that what people expect me to be?* I wondered. *I could never live up to that. Can't I just be me? If I don't become the next Andy Stanley, will people be deeply disappointed?* I thanked them, quickly headed to my office and shut the door. My mind and heart raced with fear, anxiety and a deep awareness of the expectations others were placing on me. I was scared.

Over the next several months my wife and I came to a clear awareness that becoming a senior pastor of a megachurch was not the calling God had on my life. A few months later Gary and the elders were involved in a messy struggle. After twenty years of ministry he left, causing confusion, anger and hurt within the congregation.

In the midst of the mess Megan and I found that things were different than what we had been told during the initial interview process. The elders asked that I attend the next elder meeting and shared what next steps might look like for the church now that Gary was gone. During that meeting they asked if I had anything I wanted to share. I shared that it might be difficult to hear, as I knew that Gary was grooming me to become his successor, but I was not interested in taking the position.

They looked puzzled and asked me to clarify what I meant. I told them what Gary had told me: how the elders had asked him to, in essence, find his successor and train and equip that person to be ready to take over the leadership role of the church when he retired. The room fell awkwardly silent. One elder spoke up and said incredulously that what I had shared was the first time they had heard of such a thing regarding this succession plan.

What? Are you serious? I thought. *Then how was I hired?* My mind was racing. Completely humiliated, I asked for an explanation. The elders stated that according to the bylaws of the church Gary did not have the authority to pick his successor— the elders alone choose the senior pastor. An associate pastor told me later that had the hiring process been the decision of the other senior leaders on staff, I never would have been hired, but they had nothing to do with it. It was entirely Gary's decision.

It felt like a punch in the stomach. We had moved away from our friends, our home and our church in Colorado to be mentored by a pastor in the Philadelphia area, believing it was God's call on our lives. The senior pastor was no longer there, the vision of the church was changing significantly, and we were left wondering if we had a part to play moving forward. Being told by some remaining senior leaders of the church they would not have hired me had it been their choice pushed Megan and me over the edge. We were beside ourselves as we began to hear new details not disclosed to us during the hiring process. We felt deceived. Megan was so deeply affected she could no longer attend Sunday services.

During this time Megan and I also found out that we were unable to conceive. Infertility left a searing wound on our hearts—and it was personal for me: test results revealed I was "the problem." Infertility dug wells of grief deep into our hearts that continued to overflow. Because we had moved to a new part of the country where we hardly knew anyone, we grieved alone. Through disbelief, grief, anger, shame and back to disbelief again, we carried this burden of infertility by ourselves—and it was wearisome.

As the events at the church compounded, we knew we no longer fit within the future vision of this church. The new vision set by the remaining leaders of the church, in addition to the erosion of trust, was all that we could bear. Before moving east we had thought seriously about planting a church. We had almost joined friends in a church-planting initiative in Asia, but instead we believed God called us to this large church in the Greater Philadelphia region. Now, fully aware of the turmoil, we began to sense we were being released to plant a church in the region. We approached leadership hopeful that, despite the pain, hurt and misunderstanding, they would send us out to plant a church with their blessing. We were certain this was God's next assignment for us. The leadership of the church, however, was certain it was not. They told us—quite adamantly—that we were not to do this and that it would be sin to pursue church planting in the region.

In no way was it our desire to cultivate division. As much as we tried to communicate to leadership this type of church plant would be significantly different in philosophy and expression and would not be "competition"—and that it was not a "we're taking our ball and going to another playground" posture—it was of no use. Accusations, misunderstandings, threats and ultimatums were made, further solidifying and affirming the fact that we could not stay. In a meeting with a handful of elders on a Saturday morning they told me in no uncertain terms that I would not plant a church in the region—and if I did, my employment would be terminated within the week. They gave me the weekend to decide.

It would be impossible (and unwise) to recount all the details of what transpired. To avoid being verbose or, worse yet, divisive, I will spare you much of the details. After much prayer and reflection we communicated with the church leaders that we believed, in faith, God had called us to plant a church in the region—even if it meant giving up security and certainty.

The senior leaders declared publicly I was leading a "church split" (although less than 1 percent of the congregation joined us). Although I could not have completely understood at the time (and I am fairly certain I will never fully understand it all), I believe they interpreted this as a threat. In no way did we want that. We had no desire to cause a rift or a split. We didn't want to steal sheep from the church's flock. We did not want to rock the boat. We simply wanted to go quietly.

Despite our attempts to leave well, the church's leadership was angry and upset. As an unemployed church planter I was forced to sell our house. By God's grace we sold it quickly and moved into an eighty-five-year-old rental property in need of much repair, in the community we felt called to plant a church.

Feeling completely lonely, battered, bruised, and without a steady income, a core team, a building or even a name, we ventured out to plant a faith community that we believed was initiated by God's prompting. After that tense Saturday morning meeting I left the church shaking. I drove to a local McDonald's and wrote in my journal:

God, what are you doing? I'm crazy to be called to plant a church. I'm 28 years old, my job will be terminated with 8 days notice, I have no financial support from a denomination or a sending church. I have no job or secure income. I am exhausted, bruised and battered from this experience and I have a mild anxiety disorder. What are you doing, God??

Defining Failure

On the surface my story may not seem like ministry failure in the traditional sense of the word. It is not laced with scandalous headlines or sexual impropriety. It did not involve an arrest or a gruesome addiction. Other pastors certainly have had it worse than I. And yet everything I felt was consistent with what failure traditionally feels like: betrayal, hurt, hopelessness, grief, loss, disillusionment, bitterness, doubt, anger, the need for survival and the gripping anxiety of wondering how we would make it. As a people pleaser I had failed to live up to the expectations others had placed on me. As a husband and as a man I had failed to live up to cultural expectations of being a man: the ability to get my wife pregnant. I had lost trust in leadership, in church and in people. And I had failed to live up to the expectations I had placed on myself. I had embraced a failure narrative that became deeply embedded in my mind. This was not the ministry trajectory others told me I was supposed to be on. I bet even Andy Stanley would be disappointed.

I left the church staff two years to the day after my hiring. That season of our lives could be summed up with one word: *loss*. Loss of a dream. Loss of the family we had envisioned. Loss of confidence in a God we thought had clearly communicated to us that we were to move to Philadelphia. Loss of a mentor. Loss of a church. Loss of an opportunity. Loss of trust in church leadership. Loss of local friends. Loss of a home, dependable salary and financial security. I was wrestled to the ground by grief, loneliness and despair. My soul was bludgeoned, dumped in the back alley and left in the dark. We call that season of our lives "the dark years." My wife (who is a counselor) believed I had dipped into depression. I lost fifteen pounds in a matter of weeks due to stress, anxiety and lack of sleep.

We had moved to Pennsylvania with great hope and palpable excitement; we now felt as if our souls were on life support. I was a complete mess. We were damaged goods. It was about all we could take. The week before we moved out of our house and into the home we would be renting, I went down to the basement when Megan was running errands for a few hours. I yelled as loudly as I could: "This is not what I signed up for in ministry, God! You are messing with my life, and I will not have any of it! How can you be a good God when this is what you do to those you call to do what you ask? I am giving up everything to follow you, God!"

Over the next several months we raised our own support, which was about half of what our salary had been previously. People told me that I was wasting my talents by moving from preaching regularly to three thousand people to now teaching a core team of about forty adults. They told me it was "bad stewardship." Anonymous hate mail from people at the former church continued to appear in our mailbox for well over a year. The hate mail from one elder's wife was not so anonymous.

Two years after leaving I believed my heart was healthy enough to reach out and ask the senior leaders of my former church to join me for lunch. I certainly did not want to come across as the hopeless victim. In fact, looking back I acknowledge that I could have handled certain situations more wisely than I did. Attempting to reconcile and be unified as brothers in Christ, I asked if we could meet in order to talk through what had happened. They accepted the invitation. I was surprised and hopeful at the possibility of reconciliation. I asked if we could allow each party to share how they truly felt. What transpired while sitting in that Italian restaurant booth further confounded and saddened me.

The anger had not been tempered. One of the pastors told me that leaving the church and starting ours was sinful—and that God would, as a result, continue to limit my small ministry, possibly for decades into the future. He said my ministry and our church were illegitimate and dishonoring to God. (As an aside, I certainly don't want to play the victim as I tell my story. I feel deeply conflicted in writing this, as it is difficult to be honest about my story and honoring to those who hurt me at the same time. I'm attempting to write more from my scars than from my wounds, as it is more hopeful and redemptive.)

As we were in the process of moving from our home to our rental, my daily commute would take me past the entrance of our former church. I noticed I had developed a pattern each time I passed the church entrance. As I approached with the building on my right, I would always conveniently look at the subdivision on the left. There was nothing particularly interesting about the subdivision across the street, and I wondered if I was doing this subconsciously in avoidance. The next time I drove by, I forced myself to look at the church and the expansive parking lot. The emotional blast was intense. All the anger, pain, hurt, misunderstanding, shattered dreams and strained relationships hit me. I pulled into the emergency lane and put on the car's flashers because I could no longer see. The tears were flowing with such force and fury that they impeded my vision. With my car idling in the emergency lane, the tears streaming down my face and my forehead resting on the steering wheel, I said something so calmly and matter-of-factly it startled me: "I have a problem. I need help." As I was finally beginning to understand the depth of my hurt and pain, I knew it was time to see a Christian counselor. It felt like my life was coming unhinged. While I can be stubborn at times, I did not allow my pride to prohibit me from getting help. I needed to stop the unraveling or I would ruin those closest to me. I realized I needed to heal. I finally had to come clean and own up to my kakorrhaphiophobia—the abnormal fear of failure. I needed to face failure head-on or it would ruin me.

The Issue Deeper Than Failure

I realized that I had to learn my identity was not tied to my failure—and, conversely, my failure was not tied to my identity. If I did not grasp this truth, I sensed I would remain enslaved. I had to begin the hard work of reminding myself, with the needed help and guidance of the Holy Spirit, that my worth was not tied up with what I did or who respected me (or who didn't respect me). I was skilled in preaching the gospel to others, but I was poor at preaching it to myself. I knew the gospel in my head, but it was not flowing through my bloodstream. I cared way too much about what people thought of me. (Sadly, in many ways I still care too much.) People's perception of my ministry failures had created a virtual prison that left me living in a terribly small cell. My soul was suffering from spiritual claustrophobia.

After several counseling sessions with Warren I walked into his low-lit office, sat on his counseling couch and declared,

"I've figured it out. I know what my deepest fear in life is—and it's not failure." "Oh, really? What is it then?" Warren asked. "Rejection. I fear rejection from others, from myself and sometimes what I perceive from God that comes after I've failed." Several sessions later I walked into Warren's office again, sat down and told him, "I was wrong. My greatest fear isn't failure. It isn't rejection. It's shame. Shame that comes when I've been rejected after I've failed."

I am a dogged perfectionist; I seek every possible tool to protect myself from all forms of shame. I began to see my shame—and my well-planned schemes to continually avoid it at all costs—had come to define much of my life. Through the patient support and guidance of my counselor, I began to understand the difference between guilt and shame. Guilt, he shared, says, "I failed," which reveals an action. Shame says, "I am a failure," which reveals issues of identity.[1]

The Strong Grip of Shame

More than six years later I sometimes bump into people from our former church and immediately feel my face turning red as the blood of shame and pain rushes to my cheeks and forehead. These people may have little or no knowledge of the situations and conversations that happened behind closed doors, but the shame-by-association triggers dredge up old memories.

I was at the gym on my day off a few months ago, drenched in sweat from my workout, and spotted someone who had a direct part in the hurt and misunderstanding. I found myself ducking down a row of treadmills in hopes of avoiding eye contact and interaction. It is embarrassing that at times I still find myself reacting this way, but it reminds me that though I've come a long way in my healing, I still have a long way to go. It still hurts.

The *Failure-Rejection-Shame* Process

I began to see how I responded in this failure-rejection-shame process, which can manifest itself in a variety of ways and with varying intensities. It might come when someone makes a scathing remark in front of our coworkers, or when our spouse rejects us when we reach out to show our love, or when a friend speaks sarcastically. When these situations occur we are tempted to run. We are in good company with the Messiah, who experienced what we experience. "He came to that which was his own, but his own did not receive him" (Jn 1:11). "Those who passed by hurled insults at him" (Mk 15:29). We, of course, remember his hauntingly desperate words, "My God, my God, why have you forsaken me?" (Mt 27:46). What is striking is that Jesus is met with silence; there is no answer to his question of desperation. Jesus was no stranger to the failure-rejection-shame experience (see fig. 1.1).

Fig. 1.1.

Psychologists and therapists tell us humans are wired to respond to crisis with a response of either fight or flight. When we fight—retaliate in some way with a harsh word, a vitriolic email, a revengeful act or, quite literally, a violent blow—we respond to our hurt by wanting to inflict hurt on others. Hurt people, we know, hurt people. Or we flee—we laugh at the joke made at our expense so others will not know we are hurt, slowly walk out of the room and shut down, emotionally withdraw or literally run in the other direction. We retreat so as not to deal with the conflict and discomfort and to avoid future opportunities to be hurt (see fig. 1.2).

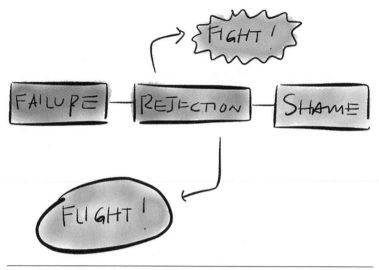

Fig. 1.2.

A Third Response

I began to wonder where the gospel was in this fight or flight process. I wondered if there might be a third way to respond. I knew the gospel never guarantees that we will not experience failure as followers of Jesus. We certainly can't expect immunity from failure, pain or suffering. It comes with the territory of our calling to follow Jesus' radical call to pick up a gruesome instrument of execution—the cross. In fact, heeding Jesus' words, when we enter into the kingdom life we are guaranteed we will experience failure. I was reminded that the gospel doesn't keep us from failing but instead transforms it into deeper meaning and a more hopeful purpose.

So what was I to do when I failed, and where might the gospel intercept this failure-rejection-shame process? In addition to fight or flight, I sensed the Lord was calling me in those times of failure and rejection to abide, to remain, to yield. Instead of retaliating and attempting to take revenge and justice into my own hands, and instead of running away, I wondered if my level of trust in the midst of the failure might grow. What if I had the *faith* and *courage* to trust God's presence in the conflict? What if I yielded to his direction? Might this be what Jesus meant when he said we should turn the other cheek or offer our tunic? What if yielding is the manifestation of trusting in and acting out my faith in Jesus and the gospel in the midst of crisis (see fig. 1.3)?

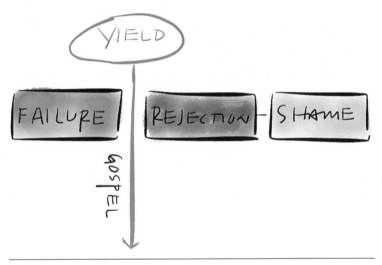

Fig. 1.3.

I was beginning to learn that this third way of yielding to God is similar to how I approach a yield sign on the road. I brake, acknowledging someone else has the right of way. When I yield, I put my foot on the brake of my life. It is an acknowledgment that God has the right of way to do as he pleases. Should the road be clear, I can proceed. When I choose this third way—yielding—the Father is beginning to move me from a place of rejection to acceptance, and from a place of shame to honor. Despite my failure to live up to some standard (which invariably leads to being rejected by others), God did not reject me. I belong to him. And somehow, in his immense compassion, he still loves me (see fig. 1.4).

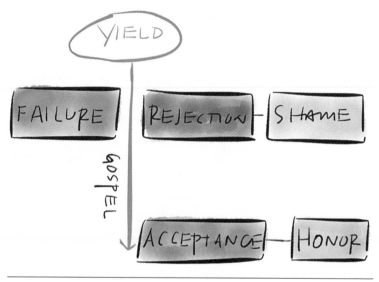

Fig. 1.4.

I had to move from thinking like an orphan to thinking like an heir. Despite my perception of ministry failure, I was not rejected by the Lord. I was not experiencing a failure I would never recover from. I was experiencing an invitation to become a child again. God's desire was to treat me like an heir.

My pastor-friend Mandy told me she takes this one step further. She easily moves from thinking like a slave ("I am nothing") to thinking like a princess ("I am everything"). When the gospel truly sets her free as she wrestles with her feelings of failure, Mandy thinks much more like an heir ("My Father is everything, which gives me value and worth"). Those precious and unfortunately all-too-rare moments in my life when I actually do yield to God's purposes are when I am ultimately free.

The Open Invitation

The crisis of failure is a fork in the road: it has the potential to transform or destroy. I was beginning to see my failure as an invitation to strengthen my faith in the Father and be called into a deeper, more intimate relationship with him if only I would accept that invitation. And when I accept, I begin to step into freedom.

It's been said that true freedom in Christ is when we have nothing to hide, nothing to lose and nothing to prove.[2] We have nothing to hide because Jesus has already covered our sin. We have nothing to lose because we are already committed to denying ourselves and picking up our cross in our pursuit of Christ. And we have nothing to prove because Christ has already taken care of it—all our sin and selfish ambitions, vain desires and self-glorifying dreams.

This downward mobility of a life hidden in Christ leads us in a direction and on a trajectory counter to the esteemed goals of our culture. We may fail, but it does not define us. We may fail, but we are loved anyway. We may fail, but we are accepted by God, who has taken our failures upon himself. We may fail, but we are invited to be an honored child of the King.

We learn this from Sunday school to seminary. We preach this. Imagine if we actually embraced this at the core of our being. The pressure is off. The invitation from Jesus still stands. There truly is nothing to hide, nothing to lose and nothing to prove.

2

SUCCESS

The Golden Calf of the American Church

[As pastors,] we are unnecessary to what congregations insist that we must do and be: as the experts who help them stay ahead of the competition. Congregations want pastors who will lead them in the world of religious competition and provide a safe alternative to the world's ways. . . . They want a pastor they can follow so they won't have to bother with following Jesus anymore. . . . [Don't forget:] everything depends upon God, so we are unnecessary. God nevertheless uses us, so let us each and together rediscover our call.

Eugene Peterson and Marva Dawn,
The Unnecessary Pastor

Remember, dear brothers and sisters, that few of you were wise in the world's eyes or powerful or wealthy when God called you. Instead, God chose things that world considers foolish in order to shame those who think they are wise. And he chose things that are powerless to shame those who are powerful. God chose things despised by the world, things counted as nothing at all, and used them to bring to nothing what the world considered important. As a result, no one can ever boast in the presence of God.

1 Corinthians 1:26-29,
New Living Translation

Ministry Stressors

Within the past week I have been on the phone with three hurting pastors. The first told me he had to shut the doors of his church plant after just fifteen months. He was wrestling through the embarrassment of awkward conversations with friends and family, and trying to untangle the knots of failure in the cords of his identity. The second pastor confessed to me that he had a severe spending addiction, which he had been hiding from his wife for several years. When he was finally caught, he admitted to tens of thousands of dollars of debt. The third pastor just wept at the pain, frustration and misunderstanding. He wept over the spiritual, relational and emotional beatings he has taken over the past several years—especially from key leaders of his church. He could no longer take the hardships and asked if I would help him write his resignation letter.

Many of us have found leading to be the most costly thing we have ever done.

We have discovered that we have been working closely with Judas and Peter.

We have found that our hearts have been worn down to a nub.

We have allowed ministry to define our identity.

We may have allowed theological prowess to define our maturity.

We have tolerated the effects of a distant marriage.

We have avoided addressing a dysfunctional relationship with our children.

We have hidden the pain of working with a distrusting board.

We have resented disgruntled congregants.

And we have admitted that we have few real friendships to speak of.

The Four Primary Categories of Ministry Failure

Stories of ministry failure are diverse. Some are because of sin, poor decisions, a lack of discretion or moral weakness. Some are moral—a clear character failure. Others are amoral—factors that were not illegal, unethical, untruthful or sinful. Despite the diversity, failure usually falls into one of four primary categories: a mighty fall, a tragic event, a slow leak or a burned-out statistic.

1. Mighty fall. Pastors have wept in front of me as they recounted their failure. As I heard some of these heinous stories I wondered if I might throw up. Mighty falls may include a sexual or emotional affair, illegal activity or embezzlement of church funds. They usually involve a sometimes years-long secret that finally is exposed. They are almost entirely moral failures that can rip families apart and leave entire congregations in shock and disbelief.

2. Tragic event. Tragic events often are not sinful, but they often are sudden and tragic. They mark leaders for years, if not for the rest of their lives. It may include the news of a spouse's cancer that took his or her life within a matter of months, a shocking termination that seemed to come out of nowhere or searing betrayal by close friends. People drown in shock, unable to come up for air, expending all the energy they can muster to try to get their heads above water. Normally other people initiate these events, and pastors are on the receiving end. More often than not, these are amoral failures.

3. Slow leak. Instead of a sudden collapse or horrifying news, some failure is the result of a subtle wearing down of the soul. Slow leaks are the constant drips of discouragement. It may include the unending barrage of negativity from an elder board, depression, disillusionment or severe resentment when thinking about how one's life and ministry has turned out. It is spiritual pneumonia— you're not dead but you experience labored breathing.

Don, a pastor in his late fifties who serves at a rural Indiana church, told me, "I've served my church for the past twenty-seven years and I've grown that church from 150 to 24 people. And the treasurer called last week and told me that we will run out of money in August. It looks like we'll have to shut our doors for good. What do I have to show for my life after almost three decades of serving God?" His face was covered with anger, confusion and resentment, but mostly Don looked resigned to the fact. His soul, it seemed, had given up the fight. He was merely existing.

Slow leaks can be either moral or amoral, but they are never sudden.

4. Burned-out statistic. Often pastors' schedules are nothing more than jumping from one crisis to the next. The treadmill is continually cranked up to higher speeds—no matter how tired the pastor may feel—until eventually the system overloads and then shuts down.

The landscape of ministry in North America is not pretty. Various surveys have reported haunting data regarding pastoral burnout:

- 1,500 pastors leave the ministry for good each month due to burnout or contention in their churches.[1]

- 50 percent of pastors' marriages end in divorce.[2]

- 80 percent of pastors (and 84 percent of their spouses) are discouraged in their role as pastors.[3]

- 40 percent of pastors seriously considered leaving the pastorate in the past three months.[4]

- Pastors who work fewer than 50 hours a week are 35 percent more likely to be terminated.[5]

- For every 20 pastors who go into ministry only one retires from the ministry.[6]

- 80 percent of pastors report ministry adversely affected their families.[7]

- 50 percent of pastors say they are unable to meet the demands of their job and are so discouraged that they would leave the ministry if they could, but have no other way of making a living.[8]

- 25 percent of pastors have been forced out or fired from their ministry at least once.[9]

- 90 percent of pastors say they were inadequately trained to cope with their job.[10]

- 45 percent of pastors say they've experienced depression or burnout to the extent that they need to take a leave of absence.[11]

- Almost 40 percent of pastors polled said they have had an extramarital affair since beginning their ministry.[12]

- Of 1,050 pastors surveyed by the Schaeffer Institute, every one of them—100 percent—had a close associate or friend from seminary who had left the ministry because of burnout, conflict in their church, or from a moral failure.[13]

- 37 percent of pastors admit Internet pornography is a current struggle.[14]

- 70 percent of pastors say they do not have a single close friend.[15]

- 70 percent of pastors say they have a lower self-esteem than when they entered the ministry.[16]

- Denominational health insurance agencies report that medical costs for clergy are higher than for any other professional group.[17]

- Additionally, the Alban Institute published a report finding that of their sample group, 62 percent of pastors reported having little spiritual life.[18]

Ministry can be brutal.

Defining Ministry Success

Before we talk about failure, we must first briefly discuss success and the current expectations that exist in many North American churches. Many pastors feel lost. One of the most recurring desires we hear among pastors is a longing for a clear metric of success—and of failure—rooted not in cultural understandings but in gospel reality. They feel sky-high expectations and unbearable pressures, and believe that it is impossible to meet the demands so many place on them.

The culture of success has become so pervasive in the church that the temptation to strive for "success" is difficult to resist. A few weeks ago a friend handed me a recent issue of a well-recognized ministry magazine. In large print across the front cover it read "100 Largest and Fastest-Growing Churches in America." Each church was ranked by attendance, with pictures of smiling megachurch pastors on each page describing the secrets of their ministry success and growth. Models, methods, practical ministry tips and advice were mentioned throughout. But one thing was missing: out of all the interviews conducted only one referred to Jesus. *Only one.* What does this obvious omission reveal about the heart of the North American church? It seems that we have a great deal of unlearning to do in ministry.

It has been said that failure is our culture's unforgivable sin.[19] Many pastors long to be known and applauded. Though called to live a life hidden in Christ, many fear being an ordinary pastor. This Hollywood-ministry narrative is seductive and destructive. Justification of our pride is dangerous. We are never in more danger of glossing over our pride than when we are in the spotlight.[20]

This striving for more is in direct opposition to the life and motivation of Jesus (see Phil 2). Jesus spent approximately 90 percent of his years on earth living a scandalously normal life as a Jewish man. Even when his ministry was public he proactively sought to be away from the crowd, to not make a larger splash. In his search for relative anonymity, he often told people to tell no one of the good he had done. Pastors are in the position to mask our hearts under the guise of smooth-sounding spiritual language, justifying our lust for more and dressing up our idols to look as if they honor God. The truth is, it does not honor him—and deep down, we know it.

Annie Dillard tells a haunting story of the 1845 expedition of Sir John Franklin and 138 men on their journey to the North Pole. They anticipated a two- to three-year journey over treacherous and icy terrain, but each ship carried only a two-week supply of coal. Instead of a larger coal supply, the ships were filled with superfluous items, including a 1,200-volume library, a hand organ, numerous settings of fine china, fancy wine goblets, pastries and several sets of sterling silver with officers' initials and family crests engraved on the handles. Incredibly, they brought no protective clothing other than their official uniforms from Her Majesty's Navy.

Years later, native peoples found their frozen corpses with sleds behind them containing mostly sterling silver, china, chocolate and even a backgammon board.[21] How many of our souls are in a frozen state lying alongside ornate church buildings with thousand-member attendance rolls? I think of Jesus' piercing question, "What good is it for someone to gain the whole world, yet forfeit their soul?" (Mk 8:36). Despite the power of the cross, we are often tempted to pursue success in all the wrong ways.

We are also tempted to shrink from risk and play it safe. But we know deep down that while we desire the success of a large and vibrant church, almost all of us will refuse to take risks because we fear failure as a potential outcome.

A Stark Definition

As pastors we've seen the idolatry of charisma. The massive cultlike following of the charismatic personality derails true biblical community. This reality may not always be evident on the surface, but when present it eats away at a faith community. It creates dependence on an individual rather than Christ. Eugene Peterson, in his piercing book *The Contemplative Pastor*, writes:

> And so pastors, instead of practicing prayer, which brings people into the presence of God, enter into the practice of messiah: we will do the work of God for God, fix people up, tell them what to do, conspire in finding the shortcuts by which the long journey to the Cross can be bypassed since we all have such crowded schedules right now. People love us when we do this. It is flattering to be put in the place of God. It feels wonderful to be treated in this godlike way. And it is work that we are generally quite good at.[22]

In his early years of leadership King Saul was the model of successful spiritual leadership by every standard in the ancient world—and yet Saul's life was a disaster. He was such a disappointment that Scripture records God's regret in placing Saul in leadership. We yearn, dream and plead for leaders like Saul, and yet it saddens God's heart. Why do we tolerate this in ourselves? The truth is, we are not important in our role as pastors (see Gal 6:3-5).

Many of us work ourselves to the bone to get to a place where we can show something for our efforts. What often results is burnout—long periods of intense exposure to personal, mental, emotional and relational stress—or, as it has been described, a convenient psychological translation for spiritual death.[23] The damaging and unmistakable consequences of burnout include exhaustion, apathy, despair, numbness and depression. Often it is not a major catastrophic event that brings pastors down but the ongoing, unrelenting, oppressive stress on the treadmill of ministry, where we simply cannot keep up the pace. It may come out in a prayer of secrecy: *Lord, I'll do anything—make deliveries for UPS, sell insurance, work in a warehouse, work construction, substitute teach. I'll do anything—except ministry.*

In their book *Reclaiming God's Original Intent for the Church,* Wes Robert and Glenn Marshall ask a series of provocative questions that may give us fresh perspective on the current ministry success metric:

- Is something wrong with small churches remaining small?

- Is something incorrect if budgets do not significantly increase from year to year?

- Is something improper if we are content with the facilities that we currently own?[24]

The pressure to run a successful spiritual franchise is staggering and pervasive.

Sadly, churches have not left room for failure in their doctrine.[25] The corrosive effect of the current standard of church success wreaks havoc on our souls *and* the souls we have been called to love. The alluring reality of success in ministry is ever present and difficult to ignore. While the drive to be successful pastors can be easily veiled in spiritual language, if we drill down a bit deeper we begin to see that it is nothing more than a glossy coating on the spirit of self-glorification. Scripture calls this selfish ambition.

Let me be clear here: it is not the size of a church's budget, square footage or average attendance I am criticizing, but an improper motivation behind the desire for a larger church. What drives us? Spotlight and recognition? Influence over thousands? Power that comes with a title? Or would we be content with a downward movement of faithful servanthood, even if it meant obscurity?

Again, large churches are not the problem. No, the deep longings and dark motivations of our hearts to pastor a large church and what that might bring us is the problem. The issue with longing for successful ministry is that models and methods motivate much of it. Unfortunately, in our current church conferences and leadership discussions those on the stage spend little time around issues of faith, dependence on the Spirit through prayer, dying to self and the ongoing spiritual development of our character—all things that mattered deeply to Jesus. When we are motivated by method and technique, we can easily find ourselves bowing at the feet of efficiency, power and progress—even if it is ever so subtle.

The story of Moses recorded in Numbers 20 displays God's way of addressing faith. Moses' lack of trust in God led him to strike the rock with his staff. Why did he do this when God told him in no uncertain terms not to do it? Because striking the rock had worked before.[26] It was faith in trusted methods rather than in God that angered God so much.

Methods and models certainly have a place in ministry. If used wisely, in proper context and with pure motives, they help cultivate healthy church environments. Our skeletal structure is vital to the health of our bodies. Structure isn't inherently bad, but placing our faith in structures is inexcusable. The temptation to turn structures, models and methods into something more is seductive for pastors looking for success at all costs.[27] How tempting it is to reach for the staff of technique and strike the rock of progress. It worked before—why would it not work again?

The Prevalence of Small Churches

Let's pause to provide some perspective. The National Congregations Study (NCS) found that of the approximately 300,000 churches in the United States, the median church had seventy-five regular attendees in worship on a Sunday morning.[28] Other studies report average weekly church attendance to be as low as fifty-eight people, and almost 180,000 churches in America (9 million worshipers) have fewer than one hundred people each Sunday. That's almost 60 percent of all churches in North America.[29] Simply put, we are a country of small churches. The problem is that we elevate a few large and spectacular churches, believing they are the norm. They aren't.

Additionally, at the other end of the spectrum, there are approximately 1,500 megachurches, constituting less than one half of one percent of churches in the United States.[30] Many of us might have believed it was the other way around. A pastor who knows almost every member's name and is familiar with most people's stories is in the vast majority of pastors in America.

For many pastors it isn't pride but insecurity that comes via comparison with larger churches. Every one of us has experienced indelible feelings of inadequacy in our lives, some more painful than others. With the expectation to be professional in our pastoral calling, inadequacy is difficult to admit. Think of the name of the degree we give graduating seminarians—*magister divinitatis*—master of divinity. What message does that send to our congregations? Have we really mastered the divine when we graduate from a theological institution? Seen by many as professional Christians paid to love Jesus, admitting weakness, ignorance or sin can be excruciating. We can become exhausted by worry when we try to live up to the expectations of others.

Lying About Seminary

Two personal experiences of ministry inadequacy have been burned into my soul. Most denominations require their pastors to have a seminary degree be ordained. Because my ministry experience has always taken place in nondenominational structures, I have not had to meet those requirements. Seminary education is a valuable tool for pastors, though one thing I learned in seminary is that you don't need to go to seminary to be a pastor.

A degree from a biblically rooted seminary can be—as it was in my own life—a meaningful experience. However, sometimes I get very uncomfortable around people who use a divinity degree (and sometimes the seminary attended) as the primary measuring stick of pastoral acumen. The book of Acts records the Pharisees (the theologically astute leaders in Israel) were amazed that the disciples (theologically uneducated men who lacked institutional ministry credibility) had not attended theological school and yet they had been in the presence of Jesus (Acts 4:13).

A few years ago I attended the commencement exercises of the seminary I graduated from. I went to hear a friend give the commencement address and to celebrate with friends who were receiving their degrees. After the service was over I bumped into Ben, an acquaintance in ministry, in the hallway and congratulated him on the Doctor of Ministry degree he had earned. After chatting for a few moments, he remembered vaguely I had also graduated from the seminary.

"How long ago did you graduate?" Ben asked with innocent curiosity.

"Oh, a while ago," I said.

"Did you get your MDiv here?" he continued.

"Oh yeah. Sure."

The conversation ended quickly as I congratulated him once more and proceeded to head home. Sadly, the truth is that I did not graduate a while ago—it had been just the year prior. It had taken me nine years to complete my seminary work, taking one class at a time as I juggled serving in ministry while trying to love my wife and young boys. (That story is addressed later in the book.)

In addition, the truth is I did not graduate with a master of divinity but with a master of arts in missional theology (what some of my classmates jokingly called "Diet MDiv"). I had lied in that conversation—twice. During the drive home I was ashamed, embarrassed and angry. *Why did I just do that? Why didn't I tell the truth? Why was I so afraid—and what was I so afraid of?* With tears in my eyes, I repented of my sin. I realized I was so insecure that I had not jumped through what many Christian leaders believe to be one of the significant hoops to be a legitimate pastor. I've often felt like the illegitimate pastor who was good enough to be a starter on the junior varsity team, but never good enough to do anything but sit at the end of the bench in my warm-ups on the varsity squad.

Feelings of Pastoral Inadequacy

Though I've been in ministry for almost a decade, I have also failed to jump through another important ministry hoop: ordination. Over the years I have had numerous people—including other ordained pastors—affirm my ministry with kind words or notes of encouragement. I have preached in various churches and denominations. Others have said they see God's hand on my life; they've specifically called out and affirmed my gifts. None of this affirmation, however, has been in the official or formal capacity of ordination. I've had a strong sense people would be more than willing to do that, but I was too insecure to bring it up. I've sensed most people assume I have already been ordained, but nobody has ever asked.

Sometimes I catch the silliness and pettiness of my thoughts, but through the years this missing piece has been difficult for me. I'm reminded of my junior varsity status. With no master of divinity, no ordination and no "Reverend" in front of my name, there are situations that trigger intense insecurity—to the point of actually believing the lies of the evil one, who whispers somewhat convincingly to my soul: *You are illegitimate. You have nothing to offer. Who do you think you are trying to pastor others? You aren't qualified for this stuff.* At times his lies seem believable.

The lies were never stronger than when I was asked to participate in my friend Evan's ordination service. Evan told me that I have had a significant impact on his life and calling as a minister of the gospel, and he wanted me to take part. The pastor who initiated and led the ordination process contacted me to solicit my involvement at Evan's request. He asked if I would sit on the ordination review committee.

I froze. While I was honored that Evan would want me to play a key role in his ordination review process, neither Evan nor the pastor knew of my nonordained status. I think they assumed it. If Evan knew the truth he would not have thought much of it. But the pastor overseeing the ordination review committee would not have asked me at all. I felt stuck.

Thinking quickly, I scheduled an appointment for the time the ordination council was to meet and sent off a reply email relaying my regrets, thanking him for his request and mentioning I would be in attendance at the service as a guest. It was not that I did not want to do it; I was convinced I would not be allowed if they had known my story. I felt like I was being deceitful. To avoid the inevitable awkwardness of the moment I hid behind manufactured busyness.

However, my attendance at the ordination service was more difficult than I imagined. Though I did not attend the ordination review process a few weeks prior, Evan requested I close the evening in prayer. As conflicted as I felt, I believed I could honor him by at least closing the evening with a brief prayer. Anybody is capable of prayer, right? I assured myself. Lots of different people pray for a variety of occasions. As I was getting dressed for the service, my heart started to race and I was already beginning to sweat through my dress shirt. I wanted to support my friend but I did not want him to know how difficult this was for me. Yet everything in me wanted to skip the service. Had I not committed to close in prayer, I would have stayed home.

When I reached the top of the stairs of the old, historic Baptist church, the pastor leading the ordination process greeted me and handed me a manila envelope. "Here, if you could, please sign this and return it to me." I moved to the back of the sanctuary, sat down and opened up the envelope. I had a hunch what it might be—and I was right. Evan's ordination certificate was in the envelope, with signatures of all the other pastors on the ordination review council with one empty line awaiting my signature.

My insecurity escalated. I opened the bulletin I received when I arrived. Halfway down the left side of the page there was time allotted in the service for ordained pastors to lay hands on Evan in prayer. I noticed the names of those who were to come forward: the ordination review council. And mine: *Rev. J.R. Briggs.* Tears welled up in my eyes. All I could think was, *I'm not a Reverend.*

I had escaped the ordination review process situation. I had maneuvered my way out of signing the ordination certificate, but I wondered how I would get out of being called to lay on hands and pray in front of the congregation. When Evan and the ordained pastors were called up front to lay on hands I quickly snuck out the back, walked downstairs and went in the men's room. In that dark, cold and cramped bathroom, I cried lonely tears.

I was grateful for Evan and confidently believed he should be affirmed in his ministry calling. I too wanted to be up front kneeling in front of a roomful of others feeling the warm hands of other pastors on my shoulders and head publicly affirming my ministry. I wasn't jealous; I was incredibly lonely. I also wanted what Evan was experiencing in that moment upstairs, not for vain recognition or attention but to have my heart know that others who have been affirmed in their God-initiated and God-given ministry also affirm mine.

I longed to have a day I could refer back to—especially when my doubts are wild and uncontrollable and the whispers from the evil one are strong and clear—or to point to a physical piece of paper to remind me that the Lord and others affirm my ministry. After wiping my tears away, I freshened up, hoping no one would see my red eyes. I walked back upstairs in time to walk to the front and lead the closing prayer. That was a difficult prayer. The service ended. We sipped punch and ate cheese and crackers in the back of the room. I was hurting. And nobody knew it.

I still had much to learn about the wild grace of Jesus who, despite our mighty falls, tragic events, slow leaks and burned-out statistics, had already affirmed me. Jesus whispers to us he uses all sorts of people for his purposes—even the nonordained. He reminds us we are not through. There is still hope. He desires for us to grasp the depth of the good news: you do not have to be Super Pastor. The pressure is off. You can take off the cape. He is still in control. This incredibly ironic, end-of-the-rope blessing is available, but only if we have the courage, patience and faith to accept it.

FAITHFULNESS

Redefining the Metric of Ministry

*Our greatest fear should not be of failure,
but of succeeding at things in life
that don't really matter.*

Francis Chan, *Crazy Love*

*If you remain in me and I in you, you will
bear much fruit; apart from me
you can do nothing.*

John 15:5

What We're Aiming At and What We're Aiming For
How you define success defines you.

Your definition of success has significant implications—not
only for you but also for those you are called to serve and lead.
And for many, how we've defined ministry success—or how we
have allowed others to define it for us—has created a dangerous
metric that is inaccurate and unsustainable.

Some of us have experienced failure clearly defined and understood as nothing less than sin. Moral indiscretion. Financial embezzlement. Purposeful deception. Broken laws. Sexual transgression. Other times, failure is not as easily defined, but it's felt, perceived or subtly implied. There may be no significant sin, but we sense something is off. We may feel like failures, others may claim we are failing in ministry or we have a gnawing sense we're not doing ministry the way it should be done.

So what does success in ministry look like? The question haunts many pastors. Much of this book focuses on the individual pastor or leader who, most likely, is wrestling with failure. This chapter, however, focuses on the systemic aspect. Certainly, more could be written than one chapter, but it is important we delve into these realities.

Maybe some of us have been told that we have failed by organizational or denominational standards. The question is, how are we to know and who establishes the metrics of success and failure? How is our church doing? Are we failing or succeeding? How am I doing—and how do I know? Pastors need a clear, robust and compelling compass for pastoral evaluation and focus.

Clearly defined ministry success often seems like a metric derived more from popular business models than from Scripture. Few people have articulated the skewed, myopic state of pastoral evaluation more clearly than Eugene Peterson. In the introduction to his book *Working the Angles*, he writes with a tone of prophetic reprimand:

> American pastors are abandoning their posts, left and right, and at an alarming rate. They are not leaving their churches and getting other jobs. Congregations still pay their salaries. Their names remain on the church stationery and they continue to appear in pulpits on Sundays. But they are

abandoning their posts, their *calling*. They have gone whoring after other gods. What they do with their time under the guise of pastoral ministry hasn't the remotest connection with what the church's pastors have done for most of twenty centuries.

A few of us are angry about it. We are angry because we have been deserted. . . . It is bitterly disappointing to enter a room full of people whom you have every reason to expect share the quest and commitments of pastoral work and find within ten minutes that they most definitely do not. They talk of images and statistics. They drop names. They discuss influence and status. Matters of God and the soul and Scripture are not grist for their mills. . . .

The pastors of America have metamorphosed into a company of shopkeepers, and the shops they keep are churches. They are preoccupied with shopkeeper's concerns—how to keep the customers happy, how to lure customers away from competitors down the street, how to package the goods so that the customers will lay out more money.

Some of them are very good shopkeepers. They attract a lot of customers, pull in great sums of money, develop splendid reputations. Yet it is still shopkeeping; religious shopkeeping, to be sure, but shopkeeping all the same. The marketing strategies of the fast-food franchise occupy the waking minds of these entrepreneurs; while asleep they dream of the kind of success that will get the attention of journalists. . . .

The biblical fact is that there are no successful churches. There are, instead, communities of sinners, gathered before God week after week in towns and villages all over the world. The Holy Spirit gathers them and does his work in them. In these communities of sinners, one of the sinners is called pastor and given a designated responsibility in the community. The pastor's responsibility is to keep the community attentive to God. It is this responsibility that is being abandoned in spades.[1]

The path of obedient, faithful ministry begins when we drop our roles as busy religious salespeople working *for* God and instead recapture our calling to live *with* him and, in turn, invite others into that life.[2] Sadly, this is increasingly difficult because often what is measured and rewarded is quite the opposite.

Paying Attention, Responding Appropriately

I quote Eugene Peterson regularly because I read him regularly; in fact, no one has marked the trajectory of my ministry more significantly than Eugene. I've had the unmistakable privilege of being mentored by him for almost a decade. We met when I was in my early twenties and serving as the emcee for an event marking the release of *The Message*. After the event I wrote him a letter; with each letter I've written he has been kind enough to write back. We've been ministry-conversation partners through the years, thanks in part to the US Postal Service.

A few summers ago he invited me to spend a few days with him and his wife, Jan, at their Montana home. While hiking together on a trail on a crisp June afternoon, I asked him what role the pastor played in the life of a congregation. He stated briefly, "To help people pay attention to God and respond appropriately."

We become what Barbara Brown Taylor calls "detectives of divinity"[3]—helping people recognize God in the world he has created. Paying attention and responding appropriately are both needed—in that order. Faithful ministry is meeting people where they are and walking with them to where God wants them to be.

The Current Metrics

The three Bs of current ministry success standards in North America are *buildings*, *bodies* and *budget*, marked by three questions: How many? How often? How much?[4] This way of thinking says, "If our facilities are large (or we are undergoing a building campaign), if our attendance is up from last year and our budget is reflecting a percentage increase, then our church is successful." What undergirds these three questions is a principle taken right out of the business management world: efficiency. The more efficiently we can address issues, tackle problems or generate numbers, the more "successful" we are.[5] It's what develops when we have a Bible in one hand and *Forbes* in the other. This focus is product oriented—and undoubtedly, money complicates this reality. There is a profound inverse correlation between progress and connection. The more efficiently we operate in ministry, the less intimacy we experience in our relationships.

In recent years the business model has been used so often by church leaders that we have forgotten there are other ways to approach ministry. The irony is that Jesus' ministry was incredibly inefficient, and yet it was significantly effective. His focus was on the kingdom—the rule and the reign of God—not on building institutions or organizations. By current success measurements, during his lifetime Jesus could have reached, healed, taught, prayed and saved more than he did. Yet even today the hopeful message of Jesus remains.

But we have swapped faithfulness and fruitfulness for progress and efficiency. We run our churches efficiently, yet we are left with an ineffective movement. We have forgotten that our primary calling is not to build a larger local church but to be active participants in the kingdom of God. Maybe our greatest failure has been placing a higher priority on the local church than on God's kingdom.

So why do we gravitate toward these three measurements: How many? How often? and How much? Because numbers are so easily identifiable. There is no subjectivity. Additionally, we've been conditioned to live as consumers—religious consumers; in turn we have helped to create a culture of Fantasy Football: Church Edition. Tim Keller writes about the psyche of church attenders, saying people will go to a church "only if (and as long as) its worship and public speaking are immediately riveting and attractive. Therefore, ministers who can create powerful religious experiences and draw large numbers of people on the power of their personal appeal are rewarded with large, growing churches."[6] This mindset is light years away from the ethos of the New Testament.

The Temptations of Pastoral Work

Henri Nouwen was more than just a Catholic priest and prolific author. He taught at Harvard Divinity School—interacting with the best and brightest minds in North America—until God called him to serve the poor at L'Arche Toronto. At L'Arche he served mentally handicapped residents who could hardly speak, could not care for themselves and were unable to perform basic functions on their own. Personal achievements, the number of books written, academic prowess, reputation and scholarly awards no longer mattered. He struggled in his new calling, but it changed his life.

His book *In the Name of Jesus* has become one of the most significant books on servant leadership and pastoral calling. Though it can be read in one sitting, it takes years to fully digest.[7] Using the temptation story of Jesus in Matthew 4, Nouwen describes the three seductive temptations to Christian leaders: the temptation to be relevant, the temptation to be spectacular and the temptation to be powerful.

The temptation to be *relevant* comes when we want to be sought out—when others desire to hear from us. Practically speaking, we think the more relevant we are in our leadership, the more people will come to our church.

The temptation to be *spectacular* comes when we are asked to don the cape and attempt something heroic. Nouwen writes, "I came to see that I had lived most of my life as a tightrope artist trying to walk on a high, thin cable from one tower to another, always waiting for the applause when I had not fallen off and broken my leg."[8]

The temptation to be *powerful* comes when we seek to control people—their thoughts, feelings, beliefs, giving, attendance and involvement. Nouwen continues, "The temptation to consider power an apt instrument for the proclamation of the Gospel is the greatest of all. We keep hearing from others, as well as saying to ourselves, that having power—provided it is used in the service of God and your fellow human beings—is a good thing."[9]

What is it about the powerful current of power, about the controlling nature of control? Power gives us an easy substitute for the hard task of love. It seems easier to be God than to love God, easier to control people than to love people, easier to own life than to love life.[10] How tragic—and how true.

Exposing Our Ministry Idols

As we explore our motivations to succeed in ministry, we must address our idols. Ministry idolatry is not often addressed, and yet it wreaks havoc and wrecks souls. Many of us are busy for God. Our schedules overflow as we seek to serve and satisfy the needs of those around us. Publicly, we claim to hate this lifestyle, and yet we are addicted. Some of us know no other way of doing it. We hate the constant barrage of demands. Yet if we are completely truthful, deep down we need it. Without the demands we would not feel needed by others. How might we feel if we are unneeded? What might that do to our identity and self-esteem? Busyness is a wolf in sheep's clothing.

Sadly, this need to be needed fuels many of our pastoral motivations. Left unchecked, people begin to need us as pastor and confidant more than they need God as Savior and Father. Feeling needed is a significant part of the pastoral identity. Many of us know this because we can sense our hearts withering each time we promote it. Idols eventually do just that: wither hearts. But there is another way available.

Numbers Appropriately Understood

As we discuss the metric of ministry it's important to clarify that numbers are not to be ignored or disregarded entirely. Again, large churches are not the issue; our failure to prioritize spiritual formation and discipleship is. James Bryan Smith at the Apprentice Institute said we have failed to move from the metric of ABC (attendance, buildings and cash) to D—discipleship.

Numbers are a part of the Scriptures. There is, of course, an entire book of our Bibles titled Numbers—but it is important to remember that the majority of that Old Testament book is made up of stories. Numbers can and should be a part of measuring health in a local congregation, but it is not the entire picture.

Numbers are important because they are rooted in the story of God and the stories of others. They influence the plot and bring texture, meaning and clarity. Stories are brought to life through relationships. Jesus told hopeful stories of the kingdom and renewed broken stories of people. Great stories are full of meaning, but they are rarely, if ever, efficient. The most important element of a success-faithfulness metric is whether our stories are synchronizing with God's story—and how they fit into the stories of others.

What determines great numbers is efficiency; what determines great stories is congruence. When our stories are congruent with God's grander story, we find fulfillment in knowing we are faithfully living into our calling. In John 15, Jesus directed his disciples to remain in him as he remained in them, which is a call to congruence. He followed up by saying, "Apart from me you can do nothing" (v. 5).

Numbers can help as a diagnostic tool of health, but they cannot be the final and exclusive report card from which we derive an accurate grade of ministry.[11] The problem arises when we put an inordinate amount of emphasis on numbers and thus downplay the role of stories. When people are seen as numbers, we rob them of their personhood and worth. A success-driven mindset in the church overemphasizes technique and results, thus putting too much pressure on pastors while undermining the importance of godly character and God's sovereignty.[12] Pastors who possess incongruent stories find themselves on a trajectory toward moral and spiritual disaster.

Are the Vegetables Ready Yet?

If a ministry success metric that prioritizes numbers is wrong, what then are we after? This requires a significant amount of wisdom, because it isn't answered with equations, formulas or spreadsheets. In short, we are called to faithfulness. Faithfulness is our metric. If the business-model approach to ministry is *product* oriented, a biblical approach to ministry is *process* oriented. With ministry, as in parenting, we're never done. People are always in process. This demands a great deal of patience and trust.

A few years ago on a Sunday afternoon in early spring, our oldest son, Carter (who was three at the time), wanted to help my wife start seeding our backyard vegetable garden. He put on his gardening boots and gloves and helped Mommy until I called him in, cleaned him up and put him down for a nap. A few hours later he woke up, opened his eyes and asked, "Daddy, are the vegetables ready yet?" I chuckled at his naive question and told him the vegetables would take several weeks before they would grow large enough for us to eat. Every inch of his face was covered with sadness; he was deeply disappointed. He wanted a product, not a process.

How often do we ask in ministry, "Are the vegetables ready yet? Is ministry growth evident? Where is the fruit?" We can become deeply disappointed when we don't see much poking through the soil—especially since the next-door neighbor's vegetables are already waist high. We can easily become impatient from a lack of results and disillusioned and discouraged from comparison.

Much of the time ministry is slow, faithful plodding. Process. But faithfulness is not an excuse to sit back and do nothing. It requires work—hard work. We don't work to earn right standing with the Father; this is not an excuse for workaholism. We work in order to be faithful to what our Father has called us to. The fine line between healthy and unhealthy pastoral work is found in the motivations of our hearts.

This hard work involves cultivating the soil for long periods of time—backbreaking work requiring faith and patience. While others may have specific job evaluations and quotas, pastors are to lean into our calling and let go of results. This is our pastoral calling—and sometimes this can be the most difficult part.

Health and Fruitfulness

There is a more descriptive and theologically accurate word than *success* in describing what we're after: *health*. Healthy organisms are designed to and expected to grow and mature. It is important to note, however, health often looks different depending on the kind of organism and its life stage.

But isn't there more than just faithfulness? What about fruitfulness as a metric of ministry success? Doesn't Jesus call us to fruitful ministry in John 15? Doesn't he expect fruitfulness from his followers? Yes, he does. But the fruit Jesus speaks of is much more personal than structural or organizational. Fruitful lives occur when people remain in the vine. Faithfulness is abiding. It might be easy to believe that faithfulness automatically leads to fruitfulness. But what about when it doesn't? What happens when pastors labor and pray and serve faithfully for years without seeing any evidence of fruit? That's Jeremiah's story. Maybe that's your story too.

Wasn't Jesus' kingdom story of the talents an affirmation from the master: "Well done, good and faithful servant" (Mt 25:21, 23)? Faithfulness isn't just who we are; it depends on our activity. Success is rooted in results. The first two servants in the parable were faithful with what God had entrusted to them (activity), and the master gave them more responsibility (results). Our calling is to live rooted in and pointed toward Jesus—and to call others to do the same. God's role is to determine the results of that activity.

Jesus' idea of fruitfulness is significantly different than the fruit that a success-driven culture expects. Maybe a countercultural life in ministry is to repudiate the idea of a metric of success that involves any results. Or maybe the standard is in being last rather than first, losing instead of winning, failing instead of succeeding.

The mother of James and John made a special request of Jesus on behalf of her boys—reserving the best seats next to Jesus. When the other ten disciples heard about the shameless request they were furious.

> Jesus called them together and said, "You know that the rulers of the Gentiles lord it over them, and their high officials exercise authority over them. Not so with you. Instead,

whoever wants to become great among you must be your
servant, and whoever wants to be first must be your slave—
just as the Son of Man did not come to be served, but to serve,
and to give his life as a ransom for many." (Mt 20:25-28)

I wonder if Jesus might say to us today, "The metrics of success-
driven ministry lord it over them. Not so with you."

The Expressions of Faithfulness

Faithfulness in our activity takes on different expressions.
Imagine you are sick and you make an appointment to see your
family doctor. Before seeing the doctor, a nurse checks your
height, weight, temperature, blood pressure and pulse. Depending on how severe your condition is, the nurse may also
take blood and urine samples for lab testing.

All of these results end up on your medical chart and are
compared with the records from your previous visits. All of these
numbers can be signs of increased or decreased health. But the
nurse would not look at you and say, "All right, you are all set.
There is no need to see the doctor. You may go." As important
as numbers are in diagnosing your health, these are not the only
tools. Your doctor still wants to see you face-to-face.

When the doctor comes into the room, he or she will probably
ask you an important question: "Tell me. How you are feeling?"
"I have a terrible cough that just will not go away," you might say,
or "I have incredible sinus pressure. I feel lousy and just want to
lie in bed all day." Your doctor may use a stethoscope and listen
to your lungs or look down your throat or check your pupils. He
or she is drawing on knowledge of the human body and experience in the relationship with you—the patient—in order to
accurately assess your condition. Finally, the doctor may write
you a prescription in hopes of seeing you return to full health.

The doctor relies on multiple forms of assessment: numbers, stories, knowledge, wisdom, experience and medicine. He or she is looking for *congruence of story*. As great and as skilled as your doctor may be, he or she is ultimately limited in healing your body. It is up to the grace of God and the mystery of the human body at the cellular level to fight disease and infection. There are other vocations where this is true. Vinedressers learn how to prune grapevines, gardeners know how much to water, and farmers know when to harvest. Pastors need wisdom as well. There is a delicate balance to using methods, forms and rhythms in ministry without learning to trust in them as surefire plans that can be used to manipulate or attempt to guarantee growth. We are dealing with people, not science projects. Trusting the Spirit to work in the lives of his people on his timetable is one of the most difficult and necessary steps to faithful living—but it is also freeing. The Spirit must do his work. It is, after all, his field and we are called to be his workers (Mt 25:14-30; Lk 10:1-12).

Is faithfulness evidenced in the stories of what God is doing in our congregation? Are people being formed and transformed by the work of the story of God in their lives? Where are people serving, what are people learning, how are people being shaped and formed in order to be a blessing to others? Where are people hearing from God, and how are they responding to these promptings? One pastor in Southern California emailed me and admitted, "We grew our church in impressive ways, but we were not anything like Jesus. We missed the point entirely." His story and the story of his people were incongruent with Jesus, whom they were called to follow.

The challenge as pastors is to possess a healthy sense of success despite the inaccurate ways we're being assessed by others. As we break out of unhealthy work habits and success measurements, it is also our responsibility to teach others (sometimes even those who lead us) what to measure and value. It takes a great deal of emotional health and confidence in God's leading. It takes a courageous pastor to stand before an elder team or committee and say humbly, "I know you'd like to see this particular measurable product, and I know I may look like a failure according to that metric, but as your pastor it's my responsibility to help us value the right things." Often such leadership induces further messes, for sure, but such is the role of pastor—to faithfully live out our true calling in the midst of the messes. We are to help people pay attention to God and respond appropriately.

The Paradox of Failure

Many of us long for the equation to a fruitful ministry. Fortunately, there is none to be found. Some will try to offer it—and may be "successful" in the eyes of others—but it won't last. Faithfulness is needed. As desirable as a formula for ministry success sounds, the fact that it does not exist is a gift, as formulas can easily become idols in a pastor's heart.

In the development of a biblically robust theology of failure, we must speak to paradox. Without paradox, failure cannot be understood appropriately. Following Jesus means we answer his call to deny ourselves, pick up our cross and follow him. As Dietrich Bonhoeffer so famously wrote, "When Christ calls a man, he bids him come and die."[13] It is an invitation to failure at the deepest level. It seems beyond radical; some might say it is ludicrous. When we live as faithful followers of Jesus, we are bound to fail—and yet this is a good thing. Failure can be a gift. Failure can be grace. Failure can yield hope. It is not contradiction; it is paradox.

The Way Forward

Surefire equations for success are not authentic. They can lead to trusting in methods more than in the Messiah. The biblically rooted evaluation metric requires trusting the Spirit further and deeper than we did last month. Though costly, it is an immense gift from God. The metric of ministry in the way of Jesus is rooted in the kingdom, which is more expansive than just a local church. It is oriented around a process, not a product. It does not ask, "Have we arrived?" Nor does it say, "Show me what you've done." Instead, it wonders if its people are moving toward or away from Jesus.

Our lives and ministries will be assessed by congruence, not efficiency. It is not found in productivity, competence or progress as much as in the development of Christlike character and coherence of our stories with the character of God. It does not find its value in the amount of our results but in the depth of our relationships. It is not found worthy through the valuation of numbers but through the evidence of stories. It is not assessed through spreadsheets but through the ability to tell stories of hope and redemption among the people we're called to love. As Nouwen writes, "The question is not: How many people take you seriously? How much are you going to accomplish? Can you show some results? But: Are you in love with Jesus?"[14]

SHAME

The Swampland of the Soul

My soul also is greatly troubled.
But you, O Lord—how long?

Psalm 6:3 (ESV)

You cannot heal what you
cannot acknowledge.

Richard Rohr,
Breathing Underwater

The Power of Vulnerability and Shame

In my ongoing attempt to develop a theology of failure, my father-in-law introduced me to the work of Brené Brown. As a researcher, a professor of social work at the University of Houston and a gifted speaker, Dr. Brown accidentally landed on two key factors that significantly influence human connection: vulnerability and shame. These areas of research fundamentally changed her perception and ultimately changed her life.

Her work provided a framework for what I had been feeling and processing, though I was unable to put words to it.[1] Her eighteen-minute talk to a room of five hundred people in June 2010 in Houston went viral, garnering several million views online. Though I am uncertain of the nature of her spiritual journey, her research is so significant in processing failure in ministry that I have shared it with many pastors.[2]

What Dr. Brown stumbled upon in her research on human interaction and connection is the very thing that unraveled it: shame. She has studied shame and its effect on humans for over a decade. Shame is the great unspoken epidemic, the force behind many forms of broken and destructive human behavior. Defined as the fear of disconnection, it is the question that asks, *Is there something about me that if other people see it or know it, will make me unworthy of connection?*

You cannot measure shame, but we certainly know its undeniable force. Shame reveals itself in various forms (guilt, manipulation, hiding, humiliation, blaming, embarrassment, etc.), and it eats perfectionists for lunch. Shame sharks smell the blood of failure in the water and swim close to the victim, anticipating attack. Shame loves to take us by the arm and usher us into darkness and hiding.

I had a shaming conversation with a close friend a few months ago. During the conversation I found myself completely covering my face for several minutes, and I was unaware I was doing so. So shamed by what was being revealed, I was literally attempting to hide. Shame is this terrible fear of being unlovable. It hates when we reach out and tell our story, because shame thrives on secrecy.

Because of its strong current, much of the pain we experience can go unaddressed. It festers, leaving us susceptible to soul infection.

Counseling professionals call shame the swampland of the soul—a place that can be visited on occasion but is a tremendously dangerous, lonely and harrowing place to live. To live in a constant state of shame is to experience hell on earth. It doesn't matter how strong our galoshes are; traveling through the swampland is never fun. And shame is not limited to a select group of people; it is universal to the human condition. The ironic nature of shame is that nobody wants to talk about it, and the less we talk about it, the more we feel it. Conversely, the more we talk about it in appropriate contexts, the less shame we feel. Shame plays two tapes: "I am not good enough" and "Who do you think you are?" What underpins shame is excruciating vulnerability. For connection to happen we have to allow ourselves to be seen—really seen. Dr. Brown's research found there is only one clear, straightforward variable that separated those who worked through their shame and those who have not: those who healthily process shame believe they are worthy of love and belonging. That'll preach.

Ironically, what keeps us from connection is our fear of being unworthy of connection. Those people who live from a deep sense of worthiness (who she calls "Wholehearted People") possess a deep sense of courage. They have the courage to be imperfect. They treat themselves with kindness and are able to show kindness to others. In the words of Jesus, they are capable of loving their neighbors as themselves. Where there is little compassion for self, there can be little compassion for others.

Research found that wholehearted people simply have the courage to be vulnerable. Courage comes from the Latin word *cur*, which means "heart." When we have courage we are able to tell the story of who we are with our whole heart. These courageous people find vulnerability to be uncomfortable, though not excruciating; instead, it's something they believe to be necessary to living. Courage. Compassion. Connection. Even with the possibility of being hurt, there is a willingness to go first, to do it anyway, to risk.

Shame and Honor in Scripture

Shame and honor are regular themes that emerge throughout the Scriptures. Jesus tells a story about honor and shame at a wedding feast (see Lk 14:7-11). The honor-shame theme is no more apparent in Scripture than in the Psalms. In our Western context we think much more with the dichotomous mindset of right and wrong than of honor and shame. Individualistically minded cultures tend to hold on to an innocence-guilt mindset while more communally oriented cultures tend toward an honor-shame perspective, as the emphasis is on relationships more than facts.[3] Though we live predominantly in an innocence-guilt culture, ministry is a relationship-centric calling in which we trade with the currency of honor and shame. How, how much and with whom we trade is incredibly significant, as it can be used easily for either good or harm. There is a fine line.

When we fail, it is nearly impossible to not feel at least a slight twinge of shame (or at least a variation of it in some form). The fact that we feel shame is evidence that we are indeed human. Shame is not inherently negative, though shaming is. If we fail to have a sense of shame, it may be said that we have no shame.[4] The rhetorical expression "Have you no shame?" leads us to see that shame, when appropriately understood, can help assist us in how we think about morality. Every culture defines shame differently—and it can be both healthy and unhealthy.

The Thai word for being shamed literally means "to tear one's face off so they appear ugly before their friends and community." With the Shoma people of Zimbabwe it means "to stomp [or wipe] your feet on my name."[5] Sometimes failure and woundedness can feel that excruciating, especially in the church. Some grow up in homes where shame, not love and respect, is the driving emotion. Shame can be a powerful tool to control and manipulate others.

I'm slowly learning that the most dangerous thing I could do after a shaming experience is to hide or bury my story. Failure's undeniable presence gets right up in our shame grill and takes us to dark places. When I experience shame, I find myself standing on the tract of land called "I'm not good enough." As pastors, if we are not willing to deal with our own shame, we can easily be tempted to use it as a veiled form of controlling others. Pastors can be skilled shame manipulators. Unfortunately, we can infer, imply or directly communicate in a way that brings shame on others in order to avoid experiencing shame ourselves. When we manipulate shame, it's simply an attempt to insulate ourselves from experiencing it further.

The Nakedness of Vulnerability

Vulnerability comes from the Latin word *vulnerare*, meaning "to wound." Quite literally it means capable of being wounded, open to attack or damage.[6] Vulnerability, when done voluntarily, is one of the most courageous acts we can engage in as humans. When we embrace vulnerability, we are on the path to maturity. Vulnerability is not weakness. We cannot avoid vulnerability; our only choice is a question of our level of engagement.[7]

Vulnerability and shame can often feel like being naked when everyone else in the room is fully clothed. While vulnerability is the core of shame, fear and the struggle for worthiness, it is also the birthplace of joy, creativity, belonging and love.[8] When we feel vulnerable, we respond in a few ways. First, we numb the feeling. What Dr. Brown found in her research is that we cannot selectively numb emotion. We cannot numb difficult feelings and refrain from numbing everything else. When we numb the bad, we also numb joy, gratitude and happiness, and then continue to look for purpose and meaning, ending up miserable.[9] When we pastors experience pain or shame, we may be tempted to open up the junk drawer of our hearts and put it away. When we refuse to deal with the pain, we actually numb everything else. Scores of pastors have described the state of their soul as being numb. Should we be surprised?

One pastor, Norm, told me of his journey of intense addiction to pornography. He felt the ongoing shame of not living up to the standards that he felt people in his church believed he should live up to. He resorted to pornography on his laptop late at night. Because of it, he felt immense shame. This shame fueled his pornography addiction further because it helped numb his emotions. This drove him to more shame, to a desire to numb and then back to pornography. It was a vicious cycle. Norm admitted to me his addiction had less to do with sex and more to do with escaping the pain and numbing his shame.

While shame is strong and at times unavoidable, we can be tempted to shift blame, spin, ignore or shrug off how deeply we can inflict our hurt on others. When we ignore our hurt and pretend that it does not impact others, we perpetuate the painful process, passing it on to those around us. We need to enter into confession and commit to working toward reconciliation. No doubt the healthiest people and the healthiest faith communities are those who realize that confession and repentance are central to a close relationship with God and others.

Letting Ourselves Be Seen

What then is the proper response to these findings about vulnerability and shame? First, as stated before, we need to let ourselves be seen—seen deeply—loving others with our whole hearts, even though there is no guarantee that we won't be hurt or experience further failure. There are few professions more open to attack by vulnerability and shame than ministry. Deep down we all want the assurance that this next time we will not be hurt, but no guarantee is available. We must simply hold to a deep trust in the Spirit to guide us, and reflect on the clear example of Christ, who showed us what it looked like to love, to be hurt and continue to love.

Second, we must commit to practice gratitude and joy, especially in moments of uncertainty, angst and stress. The last thing I want to do in stressful seasons of great uncertainty is to be thankful. Yet the Scriptures show us it's possible.

Empathy is the antidote to shame. Shame needs three things to grow exponentially: silence, secrecy and judgment. But when empathy is present, shame cannot grow. The two most powerful words we can receive from others when we are struggling are *me too*. What makes the gospel of Jesus so powerful is that it is the most humble and vulnerable gift the world has ever seen. Jesus came to earth knowing that in so doing he would be rejected and seen by others as a great failure. He experienced shame from others and loneliness in the separation from his Father. Despite knowing all of this, Jesus did it anyway. He said "me too."

It is tempting to believe we can lead others only when we are perfect. As seductive as this thought may be, the truth is (and we know the truth) perfection will never happen. Even if we could attain it, it is not what the world wants to see from us. They want to see struggle, honesty and vulnerability. We need to draw on our courage and deepen our faith once again in the One who modeled this for us by leaning wholeheartedly into vulnerability—because brokenness and authenticity honor God and inspire people.

There is a cultural price for invulnerability. At the heart of the issue is a loss of tolerance for vulnerability. Because of this, many respond in detrimental ways. First, a subtle disconnection. Similar to a low-grade fever, it will not kill us, but we will be miserable and less than ourselves. Second, we strive for perfection. We begin to believe nothing will go wrong if we simply live, look and act like what we see in the media. Perfectionism, at its core, is protectionism—a tool used to protect us from further pain. It is also an attempt control others; it is a form of idolatry. I know this. I speak from experience.

What is driving this intolerance for vulnerability in us? Scarcity—the unending expectation that we are not _____ enough.[10] The strongest statement we tell ourselves is, *We are not extraordinary enough*. We have been fed this lie and swallowed it whole: an ordinary life has become synonymous with a meaningless life. We miss what is truly important because we are on a quest for what is truly extraordinary. Grace is available in all places, but we sometimes choose to have none of it.

We tell ourselves that to be extraordinary means to be noticed, to be attractive, to be pursued and to possess power. It can be veiled ever so slightly so that very few if any notice the attempts of self-glorification. We are called not only to rise above cultural norms but to model the life of a servant. The world does not value a servant's towel wrapped around our waist, but this is our calling. However, ordinariness does not mean meaninglessness.

Perpetuating Our Busyness

We numb our lives with any number of things. For pastors one of the most accepted and encouraged yet dangerous and potentially lethal numbing agents is busyness. We work at a frenetic pace, burning the wick at both ends, believing that somehow if we work hard enough and more efficiently, we will someday achieve the necessary level of satisfaction from those we so desperately long to approve of us.

But pastors also operate with large amounts of fear. It is all too common for us to make an effort (either consciously or subconsciously) to be so busy that we never have the time to slow down and be quiet enough to listen. Type A, driven, people-pleasing perfectionists are especially prone to this temptation. Many pastors are afraid of silence. It can be incredibly intense, especially in a culture that has conditioned us to surround ourselves with perpetual noise. This busyness is not rooted in rebellion as much as in fear—fear of what we might find out about ourselves and that we might hear those searing thoughts: *I will be worthy if . . .* and *Who do you think you are anyway?*

We are often too busy because we bring it on ourselves. We seek out distraction in as many forms as it takes to avoid what needs to be addressed. Pastors regularly tell me they are petrified of silence because of what they might learn about themselves. They purposefully busy themselves to avoid hearing what they don't want to hear.

Silence and solitude are gracious gifts, but for some they can be incredibly intense, exposing deep emotions and true motivations. But we may miss the invitation of the good Shepherd. If we pay attention to the Shepherd's voice and heed the invitation of grace, we may find what is promised: rest. Vulnerability is a sharp edge, but there is nothing sharper—and more comforting—than grace.

Rejected, beaten, spit upon, humiliated, mocked, misunderstood, flogged, deserted by his closest companions, accused of wrongdoing, crucified naked on a cruel and inhumane execution device, and killed. At a moment's notice Jesus had the power to call it off and overthrow it all, but he chose to remain. His form of cosmic redemption was not control but vulnerability. When we realize that the incarnation is rooted in courageous love marked by humble vulnerability, we begin to see what God had in mind when he desired to connect deeply with his creation.

The gospel is Jesus compassionately communicating to the world "*Me too.*"

LONELINESS

The Temptation to Wear Our Masks

Even if all fall away on account
of you, I never will.

Peter (Mt 26:33)

If we refuse to take the risk of being vulnerable,
we are already half-dead.

Madeleine L'Engle, *A Stone for a Pillow*

Lonely Pastors

Pastors can be the loneliest people in the church. We are enmeshed in relationships. We know people. They want to meet with us to share their burdens. Yet many pastors feel somewhat left out. *Who are my real friends?* we think. *Who can relate to the unique position I'm in as clergy? Who will be with me to the end, through thick and thin?*

One pastor told me that although he is an extrovert, he struggles at parties and social functions. He wants to fit in and be like everyone else, enjoying the event and socializing with others, but people always seem to steer the conversation toward church matters and counseling issues. Others make lighthearted jokes about the need for everyone to behave because a member of the clergy is present. With a sense of resignation he asked me, "Where can I truly be myself? Does anybody really want me to be myself, or do they just want me to be pastor all the time? Where can I be me?"

For a place founded on grace, the church can be a place where grace seems glaringly absent. Sometimes it feels as if church-goers are skilled at shooting their wounded. Many pastors are scared stiff to be honest with their own people.

The burden of trust can sometimes feel oppressive and isolating. The unique cast of characters God entrusts to us can sometimes feel like a heavy burden: The condescending spirit of a few elders who can never admit when they are wrong. The worship pastor who responds defensively whenever feedback is given, no matter how well it is worded. The teaching pastor who delivers stirring sermons Sunday morning, but privately struggles with a pornography addiction Sunday night. The Sunday school teacher always in a position of control who will trample anyone who objects to her ideas. The key volunteer in children's ministry who incessantly criticizes your sermons, whether or not you ask for feedback. Frustration sets in with stubborn congregants who seem more interested in their comfort level than God's mission. Spiritual dryness occurs in pastors when congregants have high expectations on how they want to be fed.

Perhaps you feel like David, where the spears of authoritarian leaders are thrown your direction or an army has been raised up against you. The disconnect between our internal world and our external reality often leaves pastors feeling exhausted and emotionally numb. It's easy to feel like we are on an island. One pastor told me he felt like he was a pile of dead bones and didn't know whom he could tell.

Dan Allender reminds us that if we lead, we will at some point serve alongside of Judas and Peter—and maybe more than once. The Judases will purposefully and disparagingly betray us; the Peters will deny us, even when they think they are incapable of doing so. Betrayal and denial are a part of the human experience; not if but when—and who. "It is like looking at the ten people who serve on a committee with you and wondering, 'Who will take my words and soak them in kerosene and attempt to burn down my reputation?'"[1]

In our weakest moments the failure tape in our heads plays loudly and repeatedly. We remember the tone of the angry and power-wielding elder and the body language of the disapproving spouse. How can we forget the furrowed brow of the anxious accountant and the cancerous residue of a stinging email still sitting in our inbox? These tapes play back in meticulous detail the lacerations of criticism, the abrasions of judgment and the numerous times we have been burned by the blowtorches of people's words.

Like betrayal and denial, loneliness is a universal part of the human experience. But it seems much more intense in the lives of pastors. Despite the advantages of being in a position of influence and authority, sometimes we secretly wish for a normal life (or at least seasons of it). Leadership can usher in long seasons of agonizing loneliness.

Factors of Ministry Loneliness

Several factors lead to the loneliness. First, the astoundingly high expectations of what it means to be a pastor in our Western culture are oppressive, unattainable and unsustainable. It may not always be stated, but it's there: this week's sermon/music/worship service/counseling session/Sunday school class/Bible study better top last week's. As addressed earlier, these expectations are a result of the systemic culture of success present in many churches. Trying to one-up last week is an exhausting and unending marathon on the treadmill of ministry expectation. It feels like a lot of activity, but with no real progress—just exhaustion.

Pastors regularly admit wrestling with the thoughts of *I have no idea what I should do in this situation. I don't know how to help this person. Seminary never trained me to deal with this mess. I wonder if I'll be found out—that I am just winging it here with no confidence that this will help them.* Pastors live in fear, wringing their hands, hoping their people will be appeased and the complaints will be tempered.

The mindset can easily lead pastors to believe the most damning modern-day ministry heresy:

- If I prayed a little bit more . . .
- If I prepared my teaching a little bit longer . . .
- If I preached a little bit more passionately . . .
- If I counseled with a bit more wisdom . . .
- If I returned that phone call or email a little sooner . . .
- If I met with just one more person each day . . .
- If I _____ . . .

then our church wouldn't have so many problems and God might love me just a little bit more.

We might not openly admit this, but deep down in our hearts many of us know that we operate out of this conditional ministry posture. Our lives often betray the core message of the gospel. We may preach grace, but we end up operating out of legalistic religiosity, adding pressure on ourselves to perform and thus reinforcing our loneliness.

Second, our loneliness deepens because of our fear of confession. Many of us have deep worries (some may be well founded) of revealing who we really are to those we serve and lead. Nouwen writes that pastors are the least confessing people in the church. It may be pride or fear—or both—but they keep us in hiding.

Bryan told me that after months of soul searching, he courageously and appropriately confessed areas of personal brokenness to his congregation. He felt relieved, sensing he was modeling for his congregation the way of brokenness and grace. Over the next few days congregants complained, expressing disappointment that a pastor would share so openly. One comment dogged him: "We know you struggle with things in your life, like all of us. But you're the pastor. We want to believe you have it all together." Bryan vowed he would never open up again.

Third, sometimes our closest friends' and family members' words wound the most. We want those who know and love us most to rally around us in our times of failure. Like Job, however, our friends sometimes seem to heap it on more. Job's friends thought they were being helpful, yet they were only inflicting more wounds. We want to process the most precious parts of ourselves with the trusted friends who are trying to be helpful. But sometimes they can cause more pain by way of inaccurate theology, myopic perspective, trite responses and five-dollar answers to our million-dollar questions. Can we share how we are really feeling?

The *Almost* Truth

All of these factors leave us susceptible to one of Satan's greatest tools: the whispers of truth—plus or minus 10 percent. Satan knows we will not fall for the easily detectable lies. As pastors, we are too experienced and educated. Most effective in derailing the hearts and minds of pastors is the truth—but two ticks to the left. It is an almost truth, but it is not the truth.

But the almost truth is enough to drive us into hiding. Two significant almost truths readily available to most pastors are: *Nobody else is feeling what I'm feeling*, and *If I am a good enough pastor I will be worthy of being loved*. When we believe these almost truths, we are tempted to live dual lives. We preach God's unconditional love and yet live by religion's conditional arrangement. The natural result of believing almost truths is to reach for masks.

The Masks We Wear

Fear drives us to create and fasten masks. Masks are nothing more than emotional armor seducing us to believe we can remain unscathed. We adapt our behaviors in creative and sometimes subtle ways with motivations rooted in protecting ourselves from future exposure to pain. The deeper the fear, the more creative we can be in our mask-making abilities.

Ruth Graham, author of *In Every Pew Sits a Broken Heart,* founder of Ruth Graham Ministries, and daughter of Billy and Ruth Graham, has a passion to walk alongside of and encourage broken and wounded pastors and leaders. She told me many pastors are great image keepers. We want to make Jesus look good to others by making ourselves look good to others. We want to represent the brand well. But if we are only ministering mask-to-mask, we never experience true life change. We are simply reinforcing deceit in people who are called to bear the image of God, not keep up our images.[2] Mask making and mask wearing are forms of deception and relational manipulation— tools used to our advantage for protection. It is control.

I have asked dozens of pastors to identify the masks they wear. *The "I'm the strong one" mask.* "I have what it takes to be the super pastor you want me to be." This cultivates deep fear and pride. It fuels further dependency of the congregation on the pastor. It attempts to keep the pastor at the center of people's spiritual world and the savior they seek help from.

The "I'm theologically educated" mask. "My seminary training and mastery of biblical languages prepares me for any situation." Armed with theological knowledge, we are capable of winning almost any debate over doctrine or theology. Others are intimidated to bring things up to us (something we may actually enjoy). But knowledge is self-serving and does nothing more than puff us up; it is vanity (1 Cor 8:1). God is not interested in us acquiring an ever-expanding cognitive reservoir of theological truths that we have absolutely no intention of putting into practice.[3] We must refuse to allow ourselves to be perceived as the source of all answers.

The "I'm spiritually mature" mask. "I can handle any circumstance and will keep it together because Jesus is on my side; I am the pastor, after all." This can lead to a great deal of pressure. We attempt to be perfect and find ourselves ensnared by the endless religious cycle of trying harder.

The "I'm not hurt" mask. "God's grace is sufficient and therefore _____ [insert a few verses and spiritual clichés], and I can convince you I'm all right." One of the four-letter F-words we use regularly in our churches reinforces a lack of authenticity: *fine.* As in, "How are you doing?" "Oh, I'm fine." This exchange can be heard dozens of times Sunday morning. At times when we say this we aren't fine—and we know it. Others may know it too, but we get a pass. How often are the regular Christian clichés we use nothing more than disguises for our hurt and pain? They are not only lazy but also deceiving. Maybe most dangerous of all, we may eventually fool ourselves one day into thinking we're actually okay.

The "Do you know how much I put up with?" mask. "I deal
with so many messy people and intense issues in a given week,
I deserve a break." It has the air of victimization, arrogance and
a hint of rationalization of sin, which can lead to escapism and
destructive addictions.

The "I'm just like everyone else" mask. "I may serve as a pastor,
but I'm just a normal person like you." Being a pastor puts us in
lonely territory. At times we are tempted to want to be like
everyone else to fit in. We can go to tremendous lengths to show
people we are not as strange or irrelevant or out of touch as
others might think. It is another expression of the idol of people
pleasing and self-glorification.

The "I'm super busy" mask. "I really wish I could, but I have
too much going on right now." Busyness is one of the pastor's
most effective tools of remaining at a safe relational and emotional distance. While we feel lonely, we also want to use our
schedules to hold certain people at bay. Not only do our calendars go unchecked and unchallenged, so does our motivation.
Busyness gives us an excuse to avoid addressing those uncomfortable yet significant questions and longings. Because we are
making progress, getting things done and doing things in Jesus'
name, nobody seems to question the pace and workload.
Busyness glosses over wounds.

We have bought into the lie that if we stay busy, the truth of
who we really are will remain hidden—we will just outpace our
minds, hearts and souls.[4] We tirelessly surround ourselves with
noise and stimuli, and fill up our schedules hoping we will never
have to face what lies beneath the surface. When we model that
for our congregations, they begin to see this as acceptable behavior and thus live similarly. Plus, if we aren't busy, what will
that mean for our identity? And what might others think of us
if we aren't busy all the time?

The *"I only struggle with the little, petty sins" mask.* "I am a sinner, but I only struggle with 'respectable' sins."[5] We want people to think our brokenness and sinfulness is dark—but only generally and theoretically—and most important, that it is under control. We want people to know that we struggle with sin—but not *those* kinds of sins. When we wear the mask that we are only susceptible to small and respectable sins, we communicate to those around us a tame and tepid gospel.

The *"See how vulnerable I am" mask.* "I'm willing to share only some parts of my life with you where I'm less than perfect." This is the most difficult mask to detect—and quite possibly the most dangerous. In it, we actually use vulnerability to mask how we are really doing. It talks about vulnerability without actually being vulnerable. We control and use vulnerability for our own advantage. It keeps us from having to deal with unmet needs and gives us opportunity to strive for personal attention in veiled ways few are able to detect.

If we show enough of who we are to others, they respect us for being honest and courageous—but we are still withholding our darkest areas. It is a tireless dance of careful posturing to save face by never showing all of us. We share some of our brokenness, but just enough that people respect us and like us more than before. Show enough and we can be respected. Show too much and we get trampled. It's reputation management—vain, skillful, self-centered, carefully mapped out hypocrisy.

There are other masks pastors are tempted to reach for.[6] We reach for masks most often and most easily when our own livelihood is threatened. Masks are emotional invisibility cloaks, pastoral coping mechanisms and emotional crutches shielding us from vulnerability, numbing our pain and keeping us from the very thing we need the most: grace. Masks come off when the gospel is put on.

Loneliness and Addiction

There are different expressions but the path is similar: fear leads to mask wearing. Mask wearing leads to loneliness and isolation. Isolation often leads to addictions. John Julien, pastor of New Life Church in Philadelphia, Pennsylvania, was exposed when his cover was blown and his masks could no longer cover an addiction to alcohol. Through a supportive wife and family, gracious elders, a patient congregation, and a humble and repentant disposition to lean into the gospel, he now speaks openly of the grace he's experienced.

John shared with me, "Each time I tell my story of failure, it is a fresh lancing of the boil of my shame." Through the process he came to deeper levels of self-discovery and awareness of the idols that were present in his own life and ministry. John admitted that many congregants *want* pastors to be on the ministry pedestal. Besides being exposed in our failures by others, leading proactively through constant authentic repentance is the only other way we can take ourselves off of the pedestal.

It is easy to tell ourselves we can regain our sanity through addiction, which is self-deception at its worst. Addictions are powerful, enticing and damning. They are desperate attempts to keep us from dealing with the painful truths about ourselves. We all have addictions, but they come in varying degrees of social acceptability.

- pornography or progress
- alcohol or applause
- sex or success
- painkillers or email
- food or another late night at the church

As Tim Keller has said on multiple occasions, "You know you don't know because you don't want to know because it could be too painful."[7] Addictions try to keep us from knowing because deep down we are convinced the pain would be unbearable. At the heart of addictions is self-deception. We all have an enormous capacity to hide painful truths, especially the ones about ourselves. We can easily hide behind ministry rationalization. We can't lie to other people until we first lie to ourselves. We preach and speak truth to people, but even we can be skilled truth evaders.

We can be easily tempted to invest more in preserving our reputation and retaining our image than in dealing with the true forces and motivations of our hearts. When we hide so much under the rug, eventually we end up tripping over it. What motivates reaching for masks can be fear, insecurity, pride, a desire to escape, exhaustion and a desire to keep up the illusion we have created about ourselves.

The Temptation to Live a Split Life

We've heard of the purpose-driven life. Gordon MacDonald says pastors often lead the secret-driven life.[8] Ministry actually trains us to keep secrets: counseling sessions with couples in our office, sensitive staff information, secrets of people's past, closed-door elder meeting discussions and confidential prayer requests, to name a few. We also have our own secrets.[9] Thom Rainer, president of LifeWay Christian Resources, lists five significant secrets we refuse to tell to our congregation: My marriage is struggling, I fear my kids will grow up hating the church, I let a handful of critics control me, I often have anger toward the supportive church members who don't defend me to my critics, and I've thought about quitting several times.[10]

Wearing masks drives us to live a split life between church life and our personal life.[11] The root word of *integrity* is *integer*, meaning "one." When we possess integrity we are one person all the time. The younger son in the parable of the prodigal son lived a split life. He knows he has a father, he knows his father loves him, and yet he lives differently. But so does the older son. He knows everything in the house is his, and yet he lives as if it isn't. When we live a split life we lie to ourselves and then to others, causing cracks in the foundation.

When we root our identity and meaning in Christ, we are capable of drawing on our courage and resisting reaching for a mask. At an Epic Fail Pastors Conference in Cincinnati, Miriam, a pastor of a small congregation, shared, "God has called me to be the first one to take off the mask. I'm obedient to that, but I hate it." As excruciating as it may be, that is pure courage.

When are we most tempted to reach for our masks? When we are (or are perceived to be) judged by others, when we don't have all the answers or when others offer us clear opportunities to wear them. What may be helpful the next time we are tempted to reach for a mask is to try to identify the underlying emotions: *Am I fearful? Numb? Uncertain? Am I trying to cover the pain? Do I feel shame? If so, why? What is the source of my lack of trust in the cross, which shatters the need for a mask in the first place?*

It may be helpful to invite other trusted pastor-friends or ministry friends into these conversations. As much as we try, pastors cannot keep their own experiences of life hidden from those they wish to help.[12] If we continue to reach for masks, grace will not be essential to our lives; it will remain optional. As long as the masks remain, the loneliness remains. But when brokenness is acknowledged, grace is on the doorstep.

6

WOUNDS

Shattered Dreams, Grief and Mourning

The enemy has pursued my soul;
he has crushed my life to the ground;
he has made me sit in darkness like those long dead.
Therefore my spirit faints within me;
My heart within me is appalled.

Psalm 143:3-4 (ESV)

It is in the cellar of affliction that the good
old wine of the kingdom is stored.

Samuel Rutherford, *Letters of Samuel Rutherford*

Shattered

The following responses are from pastors who have poured out their shipwrecked souls to me over the past few years.

- You draw near to God and He walks away from you. There is no light at the end of this tunnel. It's just dark.

- Why would God give me a congregation full of people believing in Jesus but a wife who no longer does?

- I was at about my breaking point, believing God had given me enough to bear. Then my wife and I got the news that our nine-year-old daughter had leukemia. I would have quit ministry forever that week, but I had no other employable skills. So I've stayed in for the past seventeen years.

- God called me to ministry four years ago. All it has felt like is the desert.

- I have a scarlet F on my chest. It feels like a permanent F on my report card. How will I explain my past to future churches I might interview with?

- My depression is all-encompassing. I don't know how to lead a congregation well when I struggle to get out of bed each morning.

- My brother died seven years ago. It was incredibly difficult. I mean no disrespect to my brother, but his death was not as painful as the experience with my denominational leaders and bishop when we had to shut down our church.

Keith, a ministry leader, told a roomful of pastors his story as a serial adulterer. Keith had such a severe sex addiction he had been fired from three jobs because of it. He admitted to having sex with animals. Another pastor who served at a church of 2,600 people saw the average weekly attendance fall to around 150. Recently he told me his wife left him for another man he knows; he goes to sign the divorce papers at the courthouse on Tuesday.

How do we attempt to find meaning in the midst of crisis—whether sinful or not—and try to make sense of it all in the midst of the chaos? How do we pick up the pieces when our lives are in shambles? Where is the hope to be found in the rubble and wreckage? When we are hit with such pain, how do we not turn a deep shade of bitter?[1]

One well-known author and speaker told me that he has worked the past ten years with church planters and those trying to revitalize their local church, and he summarized their experiences in one word: *misery*. The apostle Paul might have described his ministry at times in a similar way (1 Cor 4:10-13). The dominating emotions I see among pastors and Christian leaders who have felt the agony of failure is anger, fear, confusion and resignation. It may be hidden, but somewhere in their stories at least one of these emotions is present.

Crisis

What about times of crisis? How shall we endure them? Crisis is that utterly horrifying feeling of being fully aware you are no longer in control of your life. The word *crisis* comes from the Greek *krisis*, meaning "to sift or separate." Many of us have been sifted. Crisis always involves two major elements: danger and shame. It's not just a threat; it presents the danger of complete and utter ruin.[2] A crisis is not a crisis unless it scares the hell out of us.

Times of crisis always mark us deeply. We hardly forget these moments. Our brains record the shipwrecks in impeccable detail. The Chinese symbol for crisis comprises two characters—one meaning "danger" and the other "opportunity." A crisis has the potential to destroy or transform, to define or redefine. In crises we either retreat in fear to protect ourselves from further emotional exposure, or we move forward in courage, opening ourselves up, knowing there may be more crises to come. On the surface, neither option is appealing.

Betrayal

At a break in one of our events, I asked Don, a pastor in the Midwest, when he felt most betrayed. He told me what happened after an elder meeting late one night. While walking to his car in the church parking lot, he was nearly physically assaulted by one of his elders. Don forced a smile as he recounted the event. I suspect he smiled because if he didn't he just might have fallen apart in front of me. The hardest part, he told me, was trying to look this elder in the eye every week after that, especially since the elder acted as if it never happened.

The life of Joseph, recorded in Genesis, astounds me. What would it be like to have my own blood brothers gang up on me, bind me and sell me to foreign slave traders, and then lie to Dad about it? Wouldn't my heart seethe with anger for several years, if not the rest of my life? Wouldn't I lie in bed at night and carefully orchestrate cruel revenge? How would I react if someone said, "Tell me about your family"?

As he rose through the ranks of the Egyptian government, Joseph was falsely accused of a sexually inappropriate relationship with a top government official's wife, suffering years in prison for a crime he never committed. How did he get up every morning while in prison and not have anger build up like plaque around his heart? How could he trust another human being? How did he stay sane through all of this? How could he stand before his brothers unrecognized and not respond with violence? If it were me, what would I want to say? What would I want to do? And how could I keep from ordering their execution? Somehow, and for some reason, God used this unimaginable story of pain and betrayal for the most ironic thing: Joseph rose to become second in command of the powerful North African country, ultimately saving thousands of people—including his own brothers. Utterly astounding.

"You Deceived Me"

And then there is the Old Testament prophet Jeremiah, whose perpetually failed pursuits are described in more detail and depth than any other prophet. God told Jeremiah that he had set him apart from birth to be a mouthpiece of truth to the nation of Israel—and yet everything he did failed.

If I were Jeremiah, how would I not become bitter when nobody listened and nobody responded to the message of repentance I was delivering out of faith-filled obedience? What would it feel like to be beaten, dragged to the center of town and placed in the stocks to be humiliated in front of everyone—all because I was doing what Yahweh had called me to do? How was Jeremiah not tempted to lie when someone asked, "What do you do for a living?" What hole would be left in my heart as I was beaten by family members, and I knew the religious scholars wanted me killed because of my ministry (Jer 26:11)? How could I recover from that?

Jeremiah picks up the pen and unleashes:

> You deceived me, LORD, and I was deceived;
> > You overpowered me and prevailed.
> I am ridiculed all day long;
> > everyone mocks me.
> Whenever I speak, I cry out
> > proclaiming violence and destruction.
> So the word of the LORD has brought me
> > insult and reproach all day long. (Jer 20:7-8)

In his deepest moments of intense emotion, he has the audacity to accuse God of lying. You might be tempted to do the same, wouldn't you? His heart takes a turn at the end of the chapter as he praises God. He gets up and communicates a message of repentance to the people again—and they throw him in a cistern to be left for dead. Babylon invaded Israel and held the city under siege for almost three years. In 587 B.C., the Babylonian army led Israel into exile six hundred miles to the north. The city of Jerusalem, once standing in splendor as the epicenter of the worship of Yahweh, was left in a burning heap of rubble. His life? Utter failure. Is it any wonder Jeremiah penned the book of Lamentations and is described as "the weeping prophet"?

The End of the Rope

What if these moments are actually expressions of harsh grace? Andrew Purves writes about the tragically redemptive reality of pastors who experience the crucifixion of their ministries—who are absolutely exasperated only to realize it was in that moment that God had full access to them and their churches. It is the moment when pastors are able to comprehend that they are incapable of forgiving sinners, raising people from the dead or bringing the kingdom of God to earth—when they realize they are the problem and often the ones in the way. These pastors were incapable of growing their churches, converting sinners or healing the dying and the sick.

Sometimes crisis and betrayal focus our perspective on the gospel by shifting from believing people need us to believing people need Jesus. Our ambition for ministry greatness need not be tamed. No, Purves writes, it needs something more severe: it needs to be killed off—crucified. This is good news, for in this moment of crisis, in this beautiful mess, we are led to experience ministry is its freest form.[3] This freedom is found when we grasp and boast to anyone willing to listen: "There is a Messiah—and I am most certainly not he."

We Know, of Course

No one has been immune to the feelings of inadequacy when we have failed to meet expectations. We need not explain what failure, rejection or abandonment feels like to others. They know it and have experienced it.

We know, of course, we live in a fallen world marred and scarred by sin. Everything we look at has had the packaging tampered with. It is not as it is intended to be. All creation groans at this reality.

We know, of course, humans are capable of making sinful and destructive decisions. These decisions have left shrapnel embedded in our hearts.

We know, of course, others have shrapnel deeply embedded in their hearts too—and it got there because we set off the explosion.

We know, of course, we are assured of failure as humans and as followers of Jesus, who told his followers to expect it.

We know, of course, in the Christian story failure precedes hope-filled redemption. Without failure, there is no need for grace. Confession—our admission of failure—is the entrance exam of the Christian faith, the threshold to the door of grace.

We know, of course, that despite knowing it, preaching it and talking about it with great regularity, we don't always believe what we say. We are tempted to believe that we do not need grace as much as everyone else.

We know, of course, that despite all of our efforts to avoid failure, we cannot. We may spend all of our days attempting to perfect our lives but cannot—and yet we continue to try.

We know, of course, shame is a powerful motivator. It leads to lives driven by shoulds, oughts, have tos and musts. We can live our lives shoulding all over ourselves.

We know, of course, failure and shame reveal. They transcend the trivial. Failure will define us, refine us or redefine us, but it will never leave us the same.

We know this, of course, but failure still lacerates our hearts and rends our souls.

The Psalms: Raw, Gritty, Naked Prayers

It is easy to read the psalms—even preach on them—without really embracing and experiencing their true essence. The psalmist does not write with any regard for political correctness—nor does he seem to care what others think of him.

I live in the northern reaches of Philadelphia, known affectionately as the City of Brotherly Love. If you have ever been to Philadelphia, you may have experienced the irony of that moniker. The people here can be brash, direct, emotional and overtly passionate. Out-of-towners often interpret us as rude people with a chip on our shoulder, a swagger to our walk and a tight-jaw resolve. Some call it the City of Brotherly Shove.

But you will always get the truth from the people of Philadelphia. Like it or not, locals will not beat around the bush or sugarcoat their thoughts. They are not polite or politically correct; neither do they temper their passions as in other parts of the country. They simply tell it like it is. I mean no disrespect to the good people of Philadelphia. I love this city. I imagine if you read this last paragraph to most Philadelphians, they would probably nod their heads proudly in agreement.

In many ways this is how I read the tone of the psalms and imagine the mindset of the psalmist: brash, blunt, direct, passionate and willing to tell you the truth in its raw form, whether you like it or not. When we are walking, limping, crawling, dragging—or being dragged—through the valley of the shadow of death, there is no need (or energy) to pray nice and polite prayers. When we pray polite prayers, it may be to disguise our lack of faith. In times of crisis the flowery language of prayer books seems trite and irrelevant. They simply will not suffice.

At an event in Colorado, Ed, a tough-nosed middle-aged pastor told his story of heartbreak and betrayal. Of all the harrowing ministry stories I have heard, Ed's was one of the worst.

He shared three prayers that were his lifeline for survival during the most difficult season of his life. The first was a reflective prayer from a fourth-century church father. The second prayer was a psalm of lament. The third prayer was by far the most significant. He stepped back from the microphone, extended his arms out to his side, looked heavenward and yelled at the top of his lungs, "GOD, WHAT THE F*** DO YOU WANT WITH ME?" The room fell silent. I looked around and saw a few dozen heads nodding in agreement. The pastor said what most everyone else had thought but few had the courage to verbalize. The psalms teach us we can pray raw prayers.

Training Wheels and Permission

The psalms are training wheels for my prayers when I don't know what or how to pray—and when the old, nice prayers no longer apply. As the late Trappist monk and spiritual guide Thomas Merton wrote, we are in need of taking possession of these psalms, to move in to them.[4]

In addition to training wheels, the psalms also gave me permission to feel and express. Calvin wrote that the psalms are the mirror to our souls. There are few, if any, emotions we feel that have not already been expressed in the psalms. Fear. Anger. Sadness. Joy. Bitterness. Doubt. Gratitude. Loneliness. Revenge. Reverence. Complaint. Compassion. It is all there. In some ways, this is incredibly comforting, reminding me I am far from alone in my feelings.

In my dark years I participated in an activity I had never tried before. I started to write poetry. I was startled by the intensity of my emotions throughout the process. It allowed a space for me to be more honest than any other place I had found before. These poems were a form of prayer I had never known. Beneath the layers of intense Philadelphia-like emotion was a desperate desire to share my inner world with my Creator. The prayer-poetry writing process felt as though I took off all my clothes, stood in front of a full-length mirror and told God, "Here I am. I've got nothing left to hide right now. And I need to give you a piece of my mind while I'm here."

Have you ever noticed that while two-thirds of the psalms are psalms of lament, hardly any of our worship songs on Sunday morning are of that genre? These lamenting psalms can be summed up in three words: *How long, God?* The psalms of lament are distress signals fired from the deck of the lost and sinking ship of our souls. Brian Zahnd said, "Psalms of lament are ways of expressing and exorcising pain so it doesn't metastasize into a demon."[5]

Some lines of the psalms are downright disturbing. The psalmist asked God to bust open the skulls of his enemies (Ps 68:21). He desired they be like stillborn children who never see the light of day (Ps 58:8). He wanted God's help in seeing them thrown into a fire and never recover (Ps 140:10). He blessed the one who took his enemies' infants and bashed them against rocks (Ps 137:9). Violent mutilation? The unbearable grief of a stillborn? The horrific death of an infant? Searing burns and death by fire? We certainly don't hear those kinds of prayers uttered during Wednesday night prayer meetings.

Lament

Few psalms are as unabashedly intense and full of unfiltered hatred as Psalm 109.

> Let his prayer be turned into sin.
> May his days be few, may his job be given to someone
>   else.
> When he is dead may his orphans be beggars.
> May he look in vain for anyone in the world to pity him.

> Let God always remember against him the sin of his
> parents.[6]

Vain. Vulgar. Hate-filled. Intense. And incredibly cathartic.
The psalms of lament are puzzling, but we dance with them,
depending on our circumstances; in good times we might be
tempted to forget them. Yet when we've hit bottom we cozy up
to them as a way of relating and receiving comfort. C. S. Lewis
writes about these intense feelings:

> Resentment, expressing itself with perfect freedom, without
> disguise, without self-consciousness, without shame—as
> few but children would express it today . . . hatred did not
> need to be disguised for the sake of social decorum or for
> fear anyone would accuse you of a neurosis. We therefore
> see it in its "wild" or natural condition.[7]

We become grateful for seeing it in its wild condition, for we
ourselves are wild.

A retired pastor asked, "With so much pain, why do we ignore
lament so much?" I sense much of it is rooted in fear. In a culture
of ramped-up success, we are afraid to admit when we are not
successful. It also brings us to an uncomfortable view of God,
and some fear the implications. It is difficult at times to live the
questions. It leaves us vulnerable. Ever noticed that every time
in your life where you've experienced significant, longstanding
growth and maturity, it included deep vulnerability? The truth
remains: it is only when we are vulnerable that we grow.

While our culture tells us to do the respectable thing and
control our emotions, the psalmist unleashes his. The psalms
have a tendency to make us uncomfortable because they bring
up difficult and sometimes unanswerable questions about God
and his world. Despite the discomfort, the psalmist does not shy

away from them. He leans into them. His range of anger, bitterness and resentment is startling. If he lived today, anger management classes and intense counseling might be a wise option. Our culture tells us such unfiltered language and intense feelings lack emotional intelligence and maturity. How can someone launch such vitriolic grenades at his enemies, who were made in the image of God? Where is the role of forgiveness that Jesus so clearly teaches? Could I get away with making some of these statements—asking God to bash my enemies' heads against the rocks and pleading they give birth to stillborn children? Would you hire someone who spoke publicly like this?

And yet David—who wrote many of these—is described as a man after God's own heart. Somehow, in the midst of the raw, blunt language, there is rooted trust. Somehow God appreciates buck-naked honesty from his kids.

I can't help but imagine the tone of the psalms of lament like that of a teenage girl yelling at her parents "I hate you!" and slamming the door of her bedroom for dramatic effect. As a parent, how do you respond to that treatment? God seems to allow this intense expression of internal turmoil.

But the psalms aren't simply a venue for emotional explosions of disillusionment and grief. Walter Brueggemann writes that the psalms of lament were a way that Israel ordered its formless grief and provided them with structure. There is form to the psalms of lament. First, a cry of complaint to God. Eventually, there is a pivot point (e.g., "Yet I will remember you"). Usually, though not always, the psalmist is able to land in the lap of God, hoping and trusting that Yahweh has heard his complaint and will choose to act. These psalms of lament—and their inherent structure—can be the frame that focuses our prayers when we're completely out of sorts. They provide form to our formless cries and shape to our shapeless complaints.

Many of the pastors who recovered and healed from failure and wounds told me the psalms felt like ointment rubbed on their wounds. They were their lifeline—their way back to wholehearted living. For some it did not mean a return to full-time ministry; it meant something better: a heart that was beating again.

The psalms are training wheels for our prayers and give us permission to speak freely. When all that is precious to us has been stripped way and we stand naked before God, there is tremendous freedom in saying, "This is who I am; now show me who you are."

7

WILDERNESS

Stumbling with Jesus in the Wasteland

Oh God, I don't love you. I don't even want to love you.
But I want to want to love you.

Teresa of Ávila, *The Interior Castle*

Therefore, since through God's mercy we have this ministry, we do not lose heart. . . .

But we have this treasure in jars of clay to show that this all-surpassing power is from God and not from us. We are hard pressed on every side, but not crushed; perplexed, but not in despair; persecuted, but not abandoned; struck down, but not destroyed. We always carry around in our body the death of Jesus, so that the life of Jesus may also be revealed in our body. . . .

Therefore we do not lose heart. Though outwardly we are wasting away, yet inwardly we are being renewed day by day. For our light and momentary troubles are achieving for us an eternal glory that far outweighs them all. So we fix our eyes not on what is seen, but on what is unseen, since what is seen is temporary, but what is unseen is eternal.

2 Corinthians 4:1, 7-10, 16-18

The Ironic Gift

Failure is a beautiful gift wrapped in an ugly package. It can be one of the most ironic gifts God offers to us—but only if we are willing to see it as such. We are fragile people in various stages of stumbling. We may be tired, but we are not dead. God is not done with us yet.

Paul's metaphor of jars of clay (2 Cor 4:7) is striking. Some translate *skeuos ostrakinos* as "earthen vessels." Paul focuses attention on the treasure. The treasure is not the container but the contents within. We are broken pots, made of dirt, possessing the hope of the good news of Jesus inside of us. It's easy to focus on the container and not what resides within. If we revere the container and disregard the contents, we become pastors with no sense of gospel truthfulness. No doubt, we are fragile souls. Despite being hard pressed in every direction, deeply perplexed, severely persecuted and painfully struck down, we still have hope because we possess something invaluable. It is the contents, not the container—like fine wine poured into Dixie Cups.

The Roundabout Way

I'm struck by the Israelites' spiritual and geographic journey into the Promised Land. God was in no particular hurry to get them out of the wilderness. Would not that be how we might understand our own spiritual journey? The pain and the hurt seem to linger—sometimes for years—without any resolution. It seems God is much more concerned about the transformation going on inside us than the circumstances going on around us.

Theologically we may be able to acknowledge that God knows what he is doing, but it is a more difficult pill to swallow when we realize he finds nothing wrong with taking his time to make sure we truly understand our pain, even if it's excruciating.[1] The spiritual journey, especially in times of failure, is never a direct route. Wildly inefficient, it can be significantly effective. During crisis God seems to give us his presence at a depth we have not experienced in times of peace and calm.

God also takes us through the wilderness the long way in order to protect us, even if we do not see it as protection. Exodus records an interesting detail in the Israelites' journey: "When Pharaoh let the people go, God did not lead them on the road through the Philistine country, though that was shorter. For God said, 'If they face war, they might change their minds and return to Egypt.' So God led the people around by the desert" (Ex 13:17-18). The roundabout way.[2] Yes, God leads us through the wilderness of our failures in a roundabout way—and he does it for our own good.

The Horror and Hope of the Wilderness

The journey through the wilderness catalyzes our spiritual fertilization. The Israelites' context is described in Deuteronomy as "the great and terrible wilderness" (Deut 8:15 NKJV). There may be no more accurate description of what we may be feeling— great and terrible. What are we to do when we are in the wilderness wondering and wandering? N. T. Wright, in his book *Reflecting the Glory*, writes that one of the frightening things about the wilderness is how many voices you hear in it. It is hard to discern between the voices—which ones are truthful and worthy of our attention and which are dangerous and should be ignored. The wilderness is the place where we wonder, *Will I make it or is this the end of the line?*

Despite the angst and anxiety, desert moments often become moments to meet God, times when we are faced with our limitations and forced to acknowledge we are unable to move forward on our own. When we are aware of our limitations, God delights in showing himself and his limitless character in ways a commentary, a conference or a seminary class never could.

But the wilderness exposes us to our vulnerability—both outside as well as inside of us. There is a great deal of barrenness, chaos and desolation in the wilderness—a vast, scorched landscape in desperate need of water. It is easy to allow the idol of self-sufficiency to creep into our view of ministry in times of success, but in the wilderness it is impossible. It is an absolute dependence on God—or it is the end.

Wilderness People

No one chooses the wilderness; the wilderness chooses us. We want to learn the lessons of the wilderness without actually experiencing it, but much to our disappointment it does not seem to work that way. The wilderness can be hot, intense and lonely, but God moves most powerfully in the wilderness. He uses it as his teacher; it is the place where we wait for him to show up and instruct. It's where we wrestle with God, which can leave us with a noticeable limp.

In many ways the exodus story is not just the story of Israel; it is our story too. In times of uncertainty and scarcity, God graciously gives manna, day-by-day provision that seems to be just enough at just the right time. We grow in the wilderness because the only way to survive is if God shows up. Here we pray "give us this day our daily bread"—and we actually mean it. We are desert people. God does not always take us out of the desert; nor does he always take the desert out of us. But he promises to give us his presence in the midst of it.

Several areas of the biblical land are wilderness—Sinai, Paran, Zin, the Negev and Judea. Some use the words *wilderness* and *desert* interchangeably. It comes from the Hebrew word *midbar*, which means "uninhabited land." The wilderness of the Scriptures can be described in one word: *harsh*. Deuteronomy 32:10 describes it as a "barren and howling wasteland."[3] It is not sandy, flat and filled with camels. It is craggy, rugged and rocky, with narrow canyons and dramatically steep rock faces. There are narrow paths that meander; walking them we have no knowledge of what might be around the bend. It is dangerous with its scorching sun, wild animals and lack of the water necessary for survival. In the wilderness we are exposed to danger and become accustomed to suffering.

The Paradox of the Wilderness

The wilderness is a place of paradox: beauty and desolation. Heartbreak and hope. Tranquility and chaos. Danger and refuge.[4] Loneliness and provision. In the wilderness some of the great people of Scripture had life-altering encounters with God: Moses complained about his leadership assignment. Elijah contemplated suicide after a dramatic manifestation of Yahweh's power with the prophets of Baal. Jacob wrestled with God and was left limping for the rest of his days. David shepherded flocks and hid in caves as a fugitive. And the nation of Israel wandered for four exhausting and frustrating decades. Abraham, Sarah, Jacob, Leah, Rachel, Isaac and Rebekah were wilderness people. Their experience was not limited to rocks. They experienced God in real, life-altering and intimate ways. They encountered God in ways I long to experience him.

Certainly, the wilderness was a place of disobedience, suffering, incessant complaining and an ongoing lack of trust. It was the location of Israel's creation and worship of a golden calf while Moses was on the mountain with God. Yet it was also a place of refuge where many experienced God in direct and indelible ways. God meets his people in the wilderness. He seems to do his best work there.

The wilderness is the place where only God provides, the place where if God does not show up, people will surely experience death. We read of stories of water pouring from a rock, manna on the earth's floor, a pillar of fire and a cloud for his people's guidance, a pole capable of healing snake bites, and a command from God to build a temporary shelter so God could live closely and intimately among his people. In the wilderness God provides for his people. He heals his people. He saves his people. And he joins his people.

Adam McHugh describes the wilderness as the mailing address for God's people.[5] The people of God learn to know and trust him like at no other time in their lives. God takes his people out of the oppressive reality of Egypt and promises them a wonderful new land, but he has to take them to the wilderness to teach them and shape them to be the people he wants them to be, different than all the other nations of the world.

We want green pastures and quiet waters; instead God sometimes ushers us into barren and desolate wastelands. Ray Vander Laan has hiked through the land countless times and now teaches the lessons of the wilderness. He said, "God's purposes for the desert is in the struggle—that we would know him more intimately."[6]

The Bedouins, a tribe of perpetual wanderers, teach us that God has given provision in the desert—we just need to know how to find it and where to look. This cannot be learned secondhand; it must be learned up close and personal. The wilderness is always one unforgettable, significant kairos moment after another.

Do we long for wilderness experiences? No. To do so would seem masochistic and delusional. However, when we experience them we can anticipate that God has a significant lesson and a desire to interact with us intimately—if we will accept the invitation. We may curse the wilderness, but one thing is undeniable: it is a vital part of our spiritual development, building us up through God's deliberate purposes.[7] The wilderness is sanctification. It is grace-laced scaffolding for our souls.

Scripture recounts that on three occasions the nation of Israel wandered in the wilderness. But don't miss this detail: the text states that God *led them into the wilderness* (Deut 8:2; Amos 2:10). If the wilderness is harsh and difficult, why would God lead his people into it? Was it to punish them? No—not initially. Israel hadn't rebelled, resisted or disobeyed yet. God led them to, in and through the wilderness from the beginning in order to shape his people toward his desires. God's desire was that his people walk his path, his way in his timing, not Israel's path (see Deut 10; Ps 23; 25). If we allow it to be, the wilderness is God's classroom in which we learn not just lessons about God but have a firsthand experience of him.

Deuteronomy 8 records that God led the Hebrews in order to teach, remind, test, shape and mold them into his distinct people. In that leading and testing, he fed them and made sure their clothes did not wear out and their feet did not swell. We often miss this incredibly important point in the wilderness narrative: God led his people into the wilderness as an act of immense grace. It was God's way of teaching his people how to walk in the way of life. Yet Israel did not see it as grace; in fact, they saw it as anything but grace. Psalm 78 gives a detailed account of the rebellion, sin and complaints of Israel toward God. God punished them because of their stubborn and hard hearts in the wilderness, but not before they entered it.

How is it that such a harsh location can bring about such tender intimacy? How can vulnerability and uncertainty usher us to learn things we never would have learned in security and comfort? Why are the most painful moments of life the times when we were closest to Jesus? A recurring theme among failed pastors is the deep hurt experienced in the wilderness and yet deep gratitude for it. Should I be surprised each time I hear this? No wonder James wrote of the surprising gift of suffering (Jas 1). Significant moments for growth abound in the wilderness. It is an environment that gives us a memorable and painful education, one we eventually may be thankful for.

Spiritual maturity is learning to embrace the wilderness as the harsh grace of God. If God does some of his best work in the wilderness, it should be no surprise that the Spirit led Jesus into the wilderness to prepare him for ministry. Why, then, are we surprised when the Spirit leads us there too? Perhaps we should expect it. Though we complain when we are in the wilderness, we might discover Jesus standing beside us the entire time, even when we have failed to notice his presence.

The great and terrible wilderness is an expression of his harsh grace for the people God loves.

8

RECOVERY

The Excruciating Process of Letting Go

Those who dive into the sea of affliction
bring up rare pearls.

Charles Spurgeon, *Spurgeon on Prayer*

Therefore, having this ministry by the mercy of God,
we do not lose heart.

2 Corinthians 4:1 (ESV)

Learning from Others

How we deal with the brokenness around us depends entirely on how we deal with the brokenness inside us. How does one recover from a ministry failure of epic proportions? What is the difference between those who come out healthy and those who don't? We have to learn to grieve. Refusing to grieve is the death sentence for our souls. We can't eliminate the hurt before we understand what that hurt has to teach us.

When King Saul died, David wrote a lament song. Strangely

enough, despite the times Saul tried to take his life and make his existence a living hell, David ordered the song be written down and taught to others. He wanted them to learn it, recite it and embrace it as their experience too (2 Sam 1:18). When we grieve and we appropriately let others in on it, we give them permission to grieve as well. When we encourage others to grieve, we teach something significant. Giving people permission to feel is one of the best gifts we can give people in order to develop gospel rhythms.

Several weeks before our first Epic Fail Pastors Conference I received a call from Stephen Burrell. Steve, a former pastor, wanted to talk to me about the upcoming event. I had fielded dozens of emails and calls from pastors who were inquiring about the upcoming event, but this one felt different. The more I heard Steve's story, the more I sensed the need to pay attention to what he was saying. Steve was a failed church planter, and part of his recovery involved returning to seminary to finalize a doctor of ministry degree. The topic of his dissertation: amoral ministry failure.

After our phone call, Steve was kind enough to send me a copy of his dissertation. Over the next several days I studied it intently. His research revealed the patterns of pastors who recovered from amoral failure—and those who did not. It was one of the largest compilations of research on the patterns of recovery of failed pastors. It also included dozens of stories of pastors' journeys through grief.

Though not knowing Steve very long, our team extended an invitation to him to speak at our upcoming event, but we could offer him no speaking honorarium. Our team wondered if he would accept the invitation, especially since the event was just a few weeks away. A few days later Steve got back to us, accepting the invitation.

Sharing research at a pastors' conference (especially research on failure) and attempting to make it interesting can be a difficult task. However, slotting Steve to share his research after lunch on the second day of the conference took the risk to a new level. I had braced myself for a sluggish and mentally tired audience, as is normally the case when people's brains are on overload and their stomachs are full. But I was stunned. Steve did not present the research; he preached it. He spoke from deep within himself. The session was not an information dump; Steve made a deep connection with pastors by sharing his own story. The usual Q&A followed, but people lingered to ask questions long after the allotted time. Pastors thanked him profusely for sharing his work. Many said his presentation was the most significant part of the conference. Some said what Steve shared exposed areas of their lives they had been hiding for several years. Almost to the person, pastors were able to identify themselves in Steve's story and the numerous stories of those he had interviewed.

How we respond to setbacks, obstacles and failures has massive implications for our lives. In the next two chapters Steve and I will share his research and stories of how pastors worked through redemptive recovery patterns, rising from the ashes to experience health and healing. We share how pastors owned up to their parts of the failure, while letting go of what was not theirs. If you have experienced ministry failure, we hope it gives you hope on your journey of recovery.

For Steve, Sunday mornings for the past five years were predictable. Everyone in the house was up early getting ready for a busy day. He pastored a small church plant in North Dallas. When one pastors a small church plant, it involves a great amount of time and energy. Since his church met weekly in a local elementary school, he set up for the service each week and tore it all down a few hours later. It was exhausting yet exhilarating work, and his entire family was involved in every aspect of the ministry. It was wonderful.

One particular Sunday morning, however, was different. As he lay in bed, the house was silent; he had nowhere to go. No rush to get ready. No need to hurry for setup. No need to race against the clock. The then-recent economic downturn had further devastated his church's giving. In addition to other issues, the church's core members elected to stop meeting as a group and assimilate into other local congregations. The church plant he had poured his heart and soul into was now a failed church. The church he wanted to spend the rest of his ministry years building now no longer existed. After dreaming and planning for two years, and working passionately for five more, the dream ended—and he was out of ministry and out of a job.

He thought about all he had accomplished, all that had gone right and all that had gone wrong. He reflected back on the process of moving to Dallas, the friendships his family had developed, the decisions they made, the financial stress they felt and the emotional strain they endured. Steve started to get angry. Steve is not an angry person by nature, but that day was different. He felt justified in his anger. He began negotiating with God about his plan for his future. How could God allow him to fail so miserably after calling him so clearly? How could he ever trust God again? How could he trust people or love them again? Could he lead another church?

He determined he would never allow himself to trust people (or for that matter God) wholly again—at least not in the same way or the same depth. Not with the reckless abandon God used to lead him to a plant a church. He could not and would not endure the brokenness and shame of another failure. God may have called him into ministry, but from now on, Steve would place limits on his obedience to him.

Fortunately, the Spirit met him that morning in bed. When he was finished with his emotional rant, Steve realized two very important things. God had the right to call him into whatever area of ministry God chose. And Steve was in no shape to re-enter ministry—at least any time soon. He was angry, bitter, scared, hurt and in no condition to lead, especially when he was struggling to lead himself.

To assist in his recovery he spent the next eighteen months in study, self-examination, research and pastoral interviews—the sources of his dissertation. He spoke with pastors, music directors, youth pastors, evangelists, church planters and dozens of national leaders from all over the contiguous United States, asking one simple question: How does a leader recover from an amoral ministry failure?[1]

Worse Than Death

Scholars agree: a significant failure is often accompanied by grief.[2] Those going through significant failure (e.g., termination, closing a church) experience a period of deep sadness. The grief of failure is so deep that pastors say it feels worse than a death. A church planter in Virginia opened up about his family and ministry, yet when we discussed his failure as a church planter, his demeanor changed, his voice dropped, his pace slowed and then he was quiet. As he spoke of the people—the severed relationships, the immense work, the vulnerable risks—he shared that his ministry failure was worse to him than the death of a child! While some may believe his response is exaggerated, his testimony was substantiated by others' responses.

The research tracked the experiences of failure through the stages of grief recovery. Before we get into the stages of grief, know that there is no set order to the process. Your recovery process may follow a different order, miss some stages altogether or spend a significant amount of time in one or two of the stages described.

Stage 1: Denial. A worship pastor came into the lead pastor's office the Monday after an exciting and encouraging Easter weekend. They chatted about the wonderful service on Sunday. The pastor was pleased with the choir, the music and the overall worship environment. There was no indication from the tone of the meeting but the lead pastor finally got around to saying that church leadership had "decided to go in a different direction." At the end of the meeting the worship pastor was terminated. The worship pastor was unable to get his thoughts around it. How could the pastor affirm his gifts and abilities one minute and dismiss him the next? He was stunned and in disbelief.

A church planter finally had a fledgling church gaining momentum and experiencing growth. The church was growing steadily but was still in need of financial assistance from the denomination. The pastor entered his review meeting hopeful—only to discover the denominational leaders determined the three-year-old effort had cost the denomination too much money and decided to end the funding. With no outside support the church would inevitably come to an end. The pastor left the meeting confused, disheartened and in disbelief.

These stories reveal the first stage of the grieving process—denial. In this stage of grief, facts are suspended, words mean little and we are left feeling numb. We even wonder if or how we will go on. We may ask questions such as, *How could this be happening to me? Did he really just say that? Is this a dream? Can this be true? Was I just fired? Did we just close the church? Is my dream really done?*

Denial can take many shapes. For instance, a pastor may refuse to do a ministry evaluation because he or she is unwilling to face his or her ineffectiveness. Another may ignore a weakening marriage or rebellious children, denying the adverse affect of a draining ministry. Still another may deny the negative effect of grief after an amoral failure. Denial is a lot less painful than awareness, but if we remain in denial, we are left stuck in our bondage.[3] Most ministers expressed a great sense of initial shock when their ministry failed. Denial is, however, rarely a long-term problem. While the residual effects of shock may last, the denial eventually slides into the next stage.

Stage 2: Anger. As feelings of sadness grow, the second stage of grief begins—anger. We believe someone has done us a great evil. Our natural emotional response is justified indignation. A suddenly fired pastor spoke of his anger. He and his family were enjoying an evening together when they encountered a leader from his former church. The simple sight of this man caused the past three years of rage to resurface. The pastor was transported mentally to his former office and the betrayal, pain and embarrassment of that experience. This leader, currently stuck in this stage, is trapped in the pitfall of anger. Nevertheless, anger is not necessarily an expression of sin. Anger is a natural reaction to the unfairness of loss.[4] It can be a display of how much we loved something we have lost.

Grief researchers indicate that the object of a grieving person's anger does not have to be related to the circumstances, person or event. It may not be reasonable, deserved or even logical. It may be leveled at the janitor rather than the leadership team, just as a cancer patient may be angry with a doctor for the diagnosis, as if the doctor is somehow responsible. We may even unleash our rage on our kids even though they had nothing to do with the pain.

Pastors may impugn themselves for shortcomings—real or imagined. They might accuse God of not answering prayer or not working in a particular way. They may assume God favors others or he failed to come through on a particular promise. They may even blame their spouse for not possessing specific skills or for a perceived spiritual shortcoming. A pastor may become angry with those who affirmed the ministry vision in the first place. He or she may blame those original supporters for now failing to support and help—or maybe even for giving to the original vision. A failing pastor may detect and criticize shortcomings with an associate or staff member. In fact, the government, denominational leaders, church members, the economy, elders, guests, the culture, unbelievers or even an unknown obstacle can serve as viable recipients of a pastor's anger and blame. Irrationality becomes commonplace.

A pastor's family may suffer profoundly because of it. Pastors may fail to recognize the depth of their own grief as it solidifies into a spirit of hostility toward God and others. While pastors can understandably experience anger, even if the anger itself is illogical, they must not and cannot remain at this stage of grief if they are to retain a healthy soul. When pastors remain angry and refuse to forgive, the research found, this rage forms a destructive foundation for the next ministry experience.

Although many pastors experienced a general state of rage, those who were able to come out on the other side realized they must move on. They have to support their families. They need work. Without regard to the anger festering in their hearts, they begin to think about the future. How will I make money? Where will I live? What kind of boss will I work for? In what denomination am I willing to serve? While attempting to answer these difficult questions, the pastor enters another stage—bargaining.

Stage 3: Bargaining. Bargaining is an attempt to manage the chaos of the past, bring our life back into orderliness and prevent the pain of past failures from happening again. We enter into negotiations with God regarding our future and, at times, our willingness to continue in ministry.

- "God, I will not work in a church unless it has at least five hundred people."

- "God, I will never be bivocational again."

- "God, I will do anything but missionary work."

- "God, I need a good salary."

- "God, I'm done with youth ministry; I'll only accept a lead position."

The conditions are as unique and varied as each individual situation, but the propensity to negotiate with God is common. Bargaining is an attempt to retain some level of control with God. However, a near universal trait of the bargainer is dissatisfaction, with just one stipulation. For instance, the pastor who seeks a good salary will also seek good health, a larger congregation, a warm climate or maybe an agreeable church board. Another individual may require an understanding boss or an effective ministry, along with various stipulations. It is a slippery slope and the bargaining never ends—just a little more, just a little different, just one more condition.

But what if God called you to a ministry that would never grow and everyone loathed you? Would you go? And what if God wanted you to serve in a particular location for no other reason than to have his name honored? Would it be enough? Could you endure the same failure again?

God called the Old Testament prophet Ezekiel to a ministry with an immense spiritual need (Ezek 2:3). At that time in history Israel was rebelling against God. The need for truth was immediate and immense—and God chose Ezekiel. What a great opportunity: a dream ministry, chosen by God himself. Yet the ministry's end is long foretold. Ezekiel understood God's expectations and understood Israel's need. However, God then told him, "but the house of Israel will not be willing to listen to you" (Ezek 3:7 ESV). God continued, "speak to them and say to them, 'Thus says the Lord GOD,' whether they hear or refuse to hear" (v. 11). God called Ezekiel to his ministry, but told him no one would listen. Ezekiel was to present God's message regardless of Israel's response.

Ezekiel, in the contemporary definition of success, was called by God to be a failure. How could he go? What could compel Ezekiel to preach year after year in spite of his hostile reception? The answer can be found in the attitude of other biblical authors. New Testament writers regularly refer to themselves as bondservants. A bondservant does not tell the master what work he or she will or will not do, and does not determine terms or conditions. A bondservant does not demand a particular salary, a work environment, a location, a nation, a people group or a title.

During the interviews wounded pastors displayed a proclivity to bargain with their future. A gifted worship pastor in the South is not in ministry today because God failed to fulfill the pastor's conditions for the type of church, in a particular denomination and in a region of the country he demanded. Another pastor demanded a particular title and job description. Today he is not in vocational ministry. In contrast, another pastor, whose forced resignation occurred more than two decades ago, currently pastors a church a few thousand miles from where he anticipated spending the majority of his ministry years and yet is finding great fulfillment.

While we can assert our conditions in our own attempt to negotiate with God, he will most likely not meet our demands, nor will he feel the need to honor them. Jeremiah wanted a different ministry. God sent him right back to the same work. Jonah's negotiations did not turn out well. Yet, in many ways, we can relate well to Ezekiel, Jeremiah and certainly Jonah. Part of the healing and grieving process may include the clear and humble acknowledgment *I am Jonah*. When God does not answer our prayers in the time or way we expect, when we discover we will endure an amoral failure, and when we think about conversations and questions soon facing us, we can find ourselves entering the next stage.

Stage 4: Depression. Depression is the natural outgrowth of grief. It is not a sign of mental illness but a proper reaction to loss.[5] In fact, not experiencing some level of depression would be unusual under such circumstances.[6] Depression is a deep sadness. It is not a condition that needs to be fixed or something that we should expect to snap out of. Pastors who are processing an amoral failure do not need to be cheered up, prodded to smile or encouraged to look at the bright side of things. In many ways trite sayings and cliché-ridden responses only add to the heartbreak and pain.

Often the insensitive (though good-natured) attempts of others to cheer up their pastor compounds the depression. Although friends and family use guarded words at the passing of a loved one, they often fail to use discretion around those who are grieving an amoral failure.

Imagine for a moment your best friend's wife has died. You've known this friend since before his marriage and were close friends of the couple. You even prayed with your friend for his wife; despite months of prayer she passed away. Because of time and travel constraints, the first time you are able to see your friend is at the viewing before the funeral. Your friend is at the head of the casket when you walk up to him. His eyes are swollen and red, and he looks utterly exhausted. His eyes meet yours and with a growing knot in your stomach, you speak. You know he needs words of comfort and healing, so you say, "Hey, you're young. There's lots of women out there. She wasn't that good of a wife anyway. Cheer up, don't be sad—you'll find another."

To say such a thing would be reprehensible. And yet similar words have been used to comfort a pastor whose job or church had ended. People say the most inappropriate things to pastors going through an amoral failure. Often others will not recognize the depth of the pastor's sadness and the intensity of his or her emotions. Or, if they do, they will interrupt it poorly and tactlessly. Far too many pastors have been told that their call was not that good, or there are a bunch of churches out there, so cheer up, you will get another. While the remarks may be true, the words are inappropriate, harsh and unhelpful.

Unfortunately, insensitive and inappropriate remarks directed toward a leader dealing with the sadness of amoral failure are not rare. People will question a pastor's ability to sense the moving of the Holy Spirit, their heart for God, their character and ability to lead, among other things. Some will try to push the pastor into another ministry before he or she is ready. Others will encourage the minister to smile and just be happy, sometimes quoting Romans 8:28.

Sadness does not mean a pastor rejects the truth of Romans 8:28, but that he or she is experiencing the normal emotions accompanying a great loss. This depression is a *stage* of grief, not a destination.[7] As with the previous stages of grief, a person processing a great loss may fluctuate in and out of depression. However, just as the denial, bargaining or anger phases cannot be the pastor's emotional destination, neither can the depression phase. He or she must move on to the last stage of grief.

Stage 5: Acceptance. While I will address acceptance more thoroughly in chapter ten, it is important to address it here as well. It is also important to understand what acceptance is and what it is not. Acceptance is not an ecstatic feeling of joy over a failure. Hearing someone say this would cause us to think they were delusional, masochistic or deceitful. Rather, acceptance recognizes and embraces the situation and outcome as part of God's overall plan, despite the pain.

Pastors in this phase are no longer angry or bargaining with God; nor are they heartbroken. A pastor from Texas who confessed to struggling with suicidal thoughts during his recovery concluded his grief process by being willing, without reservation, to endure a similar trial if it brought him the same closeness with God. Over a considerable period of time this pastor moved through the grieving process and into acceptance.

While the first four stages of grief are fluid, the acceptance phase is static. Once people reach this point they are able to discuss the failure, experience joy and forgive those who have inflicted the pain. A pastor in the Pacific Northwest shared that he was young when he joined a church staff. He had been encouraged to go there by faithful advisers. However, after a few years, a few leading families were determined to persuade him to leave. After an extended time of internal church conflict, the pastor resigned, broken and defeated. In his pain he questioned God's call and pondered his purpose for his life. He wondered if he would ever pastor again. He wondered if he even wanted to serve in vocational ministry again. He recounted his denial, anger, bargaining, depression and ultimate acceptance.

Today, he pastors a stable and healthy congregation in New England. Shortly thereafter he attended a conference in the Midwest where, to his surprise, he bumped into a person from his former church who had hurt him deeply. The two men had a cordial conversation and parted ways. The pastor recounted how he had complete freedom from any resentment or anger. He holds no sadness or anger. Clearly, and by God's grace, he has reached the stage of acceptance.

Another failed church planter told of how he almost lost his marriage. His wife, broken by the strain, was alone, hurting and looking to escape. Leading up to the launch of the church plant everyone told him he would be successful. His family affirmed him, his sending church boasted of his talents, and his denomination was completely behind him. "If anyone can plant a church, you can," echoed through his memory as he spoke during the last service. He did not leave because the church plant failed but because his personal life was a mess.

As we talked, he shared his denial, anger and depression. He recounted the steps he took to recapture his marriage and ministry. He ended the interview verbalizing how God used the failure to reveal a better ministry path in his life and begin to repair his marriage. While he did not feign happiness over the pain, he has arrived at a place of true peace with what had transpired. By an undeniable work of God in his life, he has come to the point of acceptance.

Moving through the grieving process can be excruciating; but arriving on the other side can be deeply hopeful.

9

REENTRY

Learning to Reenter the Atmosphere

Above all else, guard your heart,
for everything you do flows from it.

Proverbs 4:23

All the world is full of suffering.
It is also full of overcoming.

Helen Keller, *The Story of My Life*

Spiritual Molting

People change when the pain of staying the same is greater than the pain of changing. Failure has a way of initiating a process of change similar to what lobsters experience throughout their lifetime. In order to grow, lobsters rid themselves of their hard, protective shells in order to grow new shells. This process is called molting. Lobsters will experience molting about twenty-five times in the first five years of their life and once a year thereafter. It is a messy, exhausting and painfully slow process.

Under pressure, the shell cracks. The lobster will lie on its side, flex the muscles in its entire body and abandon the old shell—leaving itself vulnerable.

Though exposed and susceptible to attack among the ocean's predators, a lobster is incapable of growth without the process of molting. Failure and vulnerability provide Christians with rich opportunities for growth and maturity through spiritual molting. When we are molting, we seem to be keenly aware of our risk and exposure to the harsh elements. But without molting we will remain the size of our current shell forever. Without it, our growth is stunted.[1]

Following the study of grief stages and grief recovery, Steve continued to interview pastors who had recovered from a significant amoral failure. He wanted to test his conclusions regarding failure recovery and discover the specific patterns pastors utilized to help move from denial to acceptance. He observed men and women who endured great heartbreak and injustice, yet resolved to embrace the challenges of ministry again.

The Wisdom of Failed and Wounded Pastors

At the conclusion of each interview, Steve asked pastors a final question, "What wisdom would you give others going through similar situations?" Steve was attempting to get to the root issues: How might someone mentor a pastor who endured a similar amoral failure? How would they advise a wounded pastor to prepare for the next ministry opportunity? After compiling all the answers, Steve looked for themes. Several emerged.

1. Share the experiernce. These pastors went through the grief recovery experience with someone else. When recounting stories of failure and recovery, some pastors spoke of friends who had abandoned them. They recalled the isolation, confusion, brokenness, sorrow, bitterness and anger. They expressed the need for a close companion to help them cope with the heartache. On the other hand, pastors who were coached through their failure spoke of the importance of the relationship to their recovery.

2. Have a guide. Pastors expressed the vital importance of going through the grieving process with a coach or a mentor. This coach or mentor had several significant qualities. First, he or she had a broad knowledge of ministry and the realities it entails. Often, the best coaches and mentors were those who were—or still are—in ministry. Second, the coaching was not a short-term investment in the life of the wounded pastor, and the mentor did the not offer empty and pithy platitudes. Mentors or coaches had a vibrant and wise faith in Jesus and were willing to challenge sinful or unhealthy thought patterns with the intent of leading pastors back to faithful service.[2]

The role of the mentor is vital in the recovery process. No pastor who remained stuck in the grieving process had a mentor. Additionally, the research was unable to identify a coached pastor who failed to reach the acceptance stage. In short, finding a mentor or coach is absolutely essential to healthy recovery.

Other important data emerged regarding a mentor or a coach: it should not be the pastor's spouse.[3] Pastors who poured out their feelings of hurt and anger into their spouse slowed not only their own recovery but deeply wounded their spouse. After hearing of the deep pain and wounds laid out in every detail, conversation and situation, few spouses encouraged their partner to enter the ministry again, only to have their hearts be shredded yet again.

A coach or mentor may be helpful, but for some a counselor may be better suited to process wounds. You need someone who will listen to, pray for, encourage and even correct you. Processing with wise and trustworthy friends is crucial to the recovery process. If you are unable to find a friend, find a wise Christian counselor (more on this later in chapter eleven). Whatever happens, find someone other than your spouse with whom to discuss the raw details of your wounds.

3. Take care of your family. Pastors were deliberate in addressing the needs of their family. Many pastors mentioned using the extra time (a benefit to being unceremoniously relieved of their responsibilities) to spend with their families. Hikes in the mountains or walks around town, throwing the ball, watching movies, playing board games—just being together in quality, unrushed time with little or no agenda—created a healing environment for the pastor.

A pastor from Kansas used his extra time to help his wife around the house. With additional unrushed quality time together, he was able to uncover the depth of her sadness. God used the extra time together to strengthen their marriage and bring healing to his wife, who was silently grieving.[4]

4. Grieve. They gave themselves permission and time to grieve. Rather than sweeping it under the rug or just "getting over it," the pastors who recovered well stressed the importance of giving themselves permission to grieve. One pastor recalled repeatedly pouring his hurt out to his mentor, telling the story of his pain, hurt, loss and anger over and over again. The mentor wisely allowed the pastor to express his hurt and pain, giving permission for the pastor to grieve the failure. The grieving pastor processed his grief at a pace his soul needed. Today he is in an emotionally and spiritually healthy place while pastoring a church in the Northeast.

Pastors recognized a point in time when they turned the corner, when they sensed the pain would eventually subside. However, these church leaders each acknowledged a lengthy period of grief. Quite simply, they allowed themselves the freedom to be sad and gave themselves permission to cry, to weep and to grieve. They saw the recovery process as a marathon and sought a pace that was healthy.

5. Pursue God. Pastors made a purposeful effort to pursue God in the valley, anticipating God would meet them there. When the pain of rejection and loss seemed too great to bear, when these pastors felt they had nothing left, they drew closer to God. In the deep and extended darkness of anger, bitterness, denial or bargaining they found no road to recovery. The only thing left was to draw close to God. When sleep came only after exhaustion, when financial concerns seized them before refreshment, they drew closer to God. Deep down, they were aware it was the most significant factor in their chance of healthy recovery.[5]

6. Four specific practices. Pastors revealed there were four primary rhythms that were essential to their recoveries. Though nothing new, they found them to be irreplaceable. First, they committed to continuing to read the Scriptures. Almost universally, pastors reported they spent time reading their Bible regularly. On the other hand, pastors who left church work or remained in the bargaining or anger stage of grief had little or nothing to say about their time in Scripture.

Second, they continued to pray. These were not the easy, Hallmark card prayers. These were not prayers for financial help, for a job, for revenge or for answers. Certainly, those were a part of the early process of grieving, but their prayers shifted over time. Instead, these pastors asked God to teach them mercy, love, grace and forgiveness—not in a glossy, impersonal or inauthentic kind of way. They were honest, but honorable in what they prayed. They spoke of needing God's help when facing new situations, current challenges or old enemies. They spoke of desperately asking God for a spirit of forgiveness. They talked of praying for their past ministry and their uncertain future.

Third, they spent significant time in silence and solitude. For many pastors their turning point in the recovery process occurred while in solitude with God. They weren't afraid of the silence and purposefully built space for it in their lives. There is something unique about being alone to hear the Holy Spirit speak into a wounded heart.

Fourth, the pastors attended another congregation. It seems ironic: though a local church was often the cause of their deep pain, being a part of a congregation was crucial to their recovery. Attending another church while grieving kept the pastors from a spirit of bitterness. Few had a desire to serve in any leadership or service position. In fact, they clearly discouraged other wounded pastors from any formal involvement during the recovery process. However, they did express the importance of regular attendance for grieving pastors and their families.

It may sound logical, but it is worth noting: almost all pastors who attended church found they could not attend the church where they used to serve (either because of their own emotional state, the relational awkwardness, the unwritten rules of church politics or even the direct instructions given to them from their former church). Finding another church— sometimes out of the area—was helpful to the recovery process. We often call these "out of the ZIP Code" spaces, where pastors can be largely or entirely anonymous and are allowed to be an average person again.

Being a part of the back row with no formal responsibilities during a Sunday service helped pastors be present and pay attention. Several pastors have mentioned it was the first time in years they could be fully present with God on a Sunday morning, free from official ministry responsibility. Some even admitted they loved it because it was a time of receiving, something they desperately needed in their grief. Some said they cried during worship and the sermon, hearing God speak to them and meet them where they were in their pain.

Depending on the nature of your failure, finding a church can be quite difficult. (When was the last time as a pastor you had an opportunity to look for a church that was not connected to your work?) If you are unsure where to even begin, it may be wise to attend the church where your coach or mentor attends (assuming he or she lives in the area). If that is not possible, find a church where the pastor knows you and a bit of your story, and where you are sure the church will not place expectations on you or your family to be anything other than yourselves in the grieving process.

While there is nothing new in the this list of four practices, God used these repeatedly in the lives of the failed pastors. The research clearly shows that the leaders who practiced these disciplines moved into acceptance while others who avoided these practices remained stuck in the process.

7. Be teachable. The pastors possessed a teachable posture and desired to learn from their experience. Many pastors enter a time of grief by limiting their study strictly to future failure avoidance. They want to know (1) What they did wrong and how they can avoid it. (2) Who wronged them and how they can avoid these people. (3) Whose counsel they will never follow again. They immerse themselves in leadership training, reading books and attending seminars and conferences with the driving purpose of getting it right the next time to avoid future pain and failure. While learning from past mistakes is admirable, the research reveals that this is not a necessary part of grief recovery. When healthy pastors spoke of learning from the experience, they spoke of accepting the true definition of success and failure, embracing brokenness and learning from the pain.

One pastor launched a church with heavy financial support from his family. The pastor's father relocated to assist him in the launch. The church plant closed its doors and the relationship between father and son fell apart. This pastor's father remains unable to forgive his son for shutting down the faltering church plant. With seemingly every right to be angry or bitter, the pain this pastor experienced helped him recalibrate his understanding of an accurate biblical reality of success. He learned to view his ministry through God's eyes. This pastor shared that the lessons learned about leadership, success, love and ministry made the entire experience worth the painful journey.

The advice from wounded pastors to other wounded pastors is this: Learn from your experience—not the easy lessons of second-guessing or failure avoidance, but the deep lessons of the value of brokenness.

8. Look to the future. The pastors looked toward the future with hope, even if it seemed minuscule. These pastors spoke about the future in two distinct ways: first, with a focus on the enjoyable parts of ministry, and, second, with the recognition and belief that God would use them in some capacity again in the future.

An African American church planter near Washington, D.C., consecutively launched four new churches hoping each time to see a thriving congregation develop. On all four occasions he obtained denominational support, persuaded his wife to take the risk and planted a new church. Each one closed. The devastated pastor declared this was the greatest pain of his life. In vivid detail he discussed the cause of each closure. He joyfully went on to plant a fifth church. When asked what counsel he would give to a pastor enduring a similar experience, he said, "God is not done with you. Look to the future. God has not cast you aside. God is not finished with you. He is not through with you. He will use you again."

Steve recounted that he wept when the interview was over.

Observations

During the interviews several similarities emerged. After Steve finished the interviews and compiled statements looking for common experiences, certain observations became apparent.

A seven- to fourteen-month recovery window. Each pastor who moved through the stages of grief was asked when acceptance occurred. On rare occasions some pastors moved through grief in a month's time; others were almost two years in length. However, the majority of recoveries fell within a seven- to fourteen-month window. Pastors who took longer than fourteen months were typically stuck in one of the stages of grieving. While some want grieving pastors to be ready for ministry in a few weeks, typically a pastor remained in the stages of grief for at least seven months' time.[6]

This window gives permission to grieve loss, to struggle with anger and depression, to work through bargaining, to face denial and, by God's grace, to come to the place of acceptance. It allows the necessary time to heal.[7] It's probably no coincidence that Jewish rituals set aside a full year of grieving for the death of a loved one. It helps explain why former pastors resist when a friend asks for help in a particular church ministry. Many pastors found it to be helpful to find employment outside of a church during this window because they were not ready to jump into ministry again.

Relationships with non-Christians. Connecting with those outside of the church was, by far, the most widespread and surprising observation. As each pastor told of his or her recovery and reentry into ministry, one assertion was collectively true. Each pastor developed significant relationships with non-Christians before reconnecting again to the larger Christian community.

A pastor in the state of Washington took a job at a wood-processing factory and started a Bible study with the workers. A church planter in the Midwest took a job at a seafood restaurant, enjoying lengthy conversations with his non-Christian coworkers. A Pennsylvania pastor worked at a large retail chain and found natural opportunities to share his journey with Christ with those he encountered while stocking shelves and in the break room.

Some of these pastors were not regularly attending a local church. Some had little to no connection with any Christians. Ironically, many pastors found non-Christians more honest and less judgmental. They more quickly saw pastors as people first. Some pastors were so angry at anything looking like establishment Christianity they recoiled at the very thought of serving in a church. In each case the pastor's return to ministry began with connecting with non-Christians. God seems to have creative ways to bring healing to pastors.

If you are coaching pastors who endured a significant amoral failure, resist the natural tendency to quickly draw these pastors relationally into the life of a local congregation. This seems counterintuitive to their recovery, especially since many of them found attending a church a healthy discipline. Though they attended church, a significant amount of their free time was spent with people who had no connection to church. Several pastors sought opportunities to lead a nontraditional small group of people who knew nothing about the Bible. For many, this was one of the most refreshing things they did. Ironically, some pastors were most affected by their time with non-Christians. None of the interviewed pastors were able to explain why they connected with non-Christians. In fact, no pastor set out to make relational connections outside the church; it was just part of their story.[8]

A significant and deeply meaningful "God moment." Many described a unique event—a turning point—in their recovery process. It was a time when they sensed the undeniable and healing presence of God. The Holy Spirit uniquely and graciously communicated with them that ultimately they would be all right. We call this experience the "Special God Moment." It may not be the most creative term, but who can explain in words the significant and undeniable movement of God in another's life? God moved in the deepest part of the pastor's soul. In a still, quiet voice he breathed health and healing into their brokenness. From the moment of God's moving, the pastors moved toward acceptance.

A pastor resigned from a church after a long and arduous period of tension. He loved the church and had poured a great deal of time and energy into the people. He worked for nominal compensation and went without health insurance, which affected his health because he was unable to afford necessary medications. After leaving the church he was forced to move his family into his relatives' home. He was angry, bitter and bargaining. He was in a terrible place until he experienced a Special God Moment. He attended a church conference in Dallas. He wept for six of the seven-hour trip home. He cried so long and so hard he had difficulty driving home from the airport. In the midst of the trip, in his brokenness and weeping, he sensed God. It was heart surgery. God showed up and the man had an undeniable awareness he would be okay.

The pastor who took a job at the wood-processing factory also experienced a Special God Moment. One evening he stood at a door of the factory looking out over the beautiful mountains. He was thinking about his time at seminary, his dream of ministry with his wife and his horribly difficult failure. As he contemplated whether he would ever serve vocationally in a church again, the Spirit showed up in an undeniably powerful way. He knew, as he went back to work, he would be okay. He knew he would learn to forgive and God would use him again. He was unable to describe the event in vivid detail—no voices, no visions and no spotlights with the "Hallelujah Chorus"—just a clear and resolute sense of God's presence in his life.

As Steve presented an abridged version of the last two chapters at the Epic Fail Conference, pastors who had held on to anger for decades began to forgive. Leaders who felt abandoned and alone in their grief sensed God's presence and wept around tables with other broken pastors. Those who had been bargaining with God began to affirm their willing to serve Christ freely without conditions in whatever form or direction that took. Steve and I believe in the Special God Moment because we've seen it happen—ironically, even as the research was presented.

Walk this road faithfully. Endure the grief with others. Learn what God is teaching you. There is a life of joy, meaning and wholeness ahead for those who process grief well.

10

ACCEPTANCE

A Kiss from God on Our Bruises

Generally, by the time you are Real . . . your hair has been loved off, and your eyes drop out and you get loose in the joints and very shabby. But these things don't matter at all, because once you are Real you can't be ugly, except to people who don't understand.

The Skin Horse, *The Velveteen Rabbit*

Whatever gain I had, I counted as loss for the sake of Christ. Indeed, I count everything as loss because of the surpassing worth of knowing Christ Jesus my Lord. For his sake I have suffered the loss of all things and count them as rubbish, in order that I may gain Christ and be found in him, not having a righteousness of my own that comes from the law, but that which comes through faith in Christ, the righteousness from God that depends on faith—that I may know him and the power of his resurrection, and may share his sufferings, becoming like him in his death, that by any means possible I may attain the resurrection from the dead.

Philippians 3:7-11 (esv)

Beauty and Brokenness

In the top drawer of my desk sit four broken pieces of green and blue stained glass. Several years ago my wife and I led a team of young adults to Manica, Mozambique, on a short-term trip. Early one morning our hosts led us on a hike up a hill, past the thatched roofs of the village to an abandoned building. At one point it was home to a thriving Catholic church, but the building was decommissioned. The pews, the altar and the all relics were gone. What remained was a cement shell with peeling white paint, rancid smells and animal feces in each of its four corners. I noticed piles of broken stained glass under each window. I presume children had broken the windows for fun. I picked up several pieces and put them in my travel bag.

As I walked by, the angle was just right to catch a magnificent view of the sun glimmering through the jagged shards of glass still attached to the windows. Despite its brokenness, its beauty was stunning. It was beautiful because of its brokenness. When we are broken, we have the potential to be beautiful because of what works through us.

We have a hauntingly large capacity to make colossal mistakes. When we demand perfection in ourselves and others, we have set ourselves up for eventual disillusionment. In many ways our failure intersects our lives and forces us to make a decision: we can become bitter or recognize it as a place of growth and maturity. We are broken stained glass. Will we be repulsed by that fact, or will we embrace it and see the beauty for what it is? If we hide the brokenness, the beauty will not be discovered; nor will it be shared with others as a source of hope.

The Blessing at the End of the Rope

Many Christian leaders fear being perceived as high maintenance. We have been conditioned to be givers, not receivers. It is much easier for us to wash the feet of others than it is to be washed. Some environments demand that we be the superpastor who has it all together, whose family is wonderful and well behaved, whose temperament and demeanor are always joyful and gracious. Yet the power of gospel truth is blunt: we are all high maintenance. We are spiritually needy. We cannot save ourselves. We make messes and cause pain. We wander and lose our way. That is why we need a God who can rescue us from ourselves. The gospel proclaims that we need help, and by accepting it we declare unabashedly, "I cannot do this life on my own." It is an acknowledgment that I cannot create a future for myself more meaningful or purposeful than God can.

The first line of the Beatitudes reads, "You're blessed when you're at the end of your rope. With less of you there's more of God and his rule" (Mt 5:3 *The Message*). I stood listening to Byron, a former pastor, share that two years prior he had been arrested in a prostitution sting. His epic failure was the front-page headline of a nationally recognized newspaper. He recounted the pain, the humiliation and the immeasurable harm his sinful decisions had—and continue to have—on his friends, his ex-wife, his children and his former congregation. Byron told me, "I wish I could take away the incredible pain and damage my sin inflicted on so many people I care about. But it was the best thing that could have happened to me at that point of my life because it brought me to the end of myself and to my beginning with Christ."

Sometimes our failure includes a lot of pain, but it doesn't always involve sin. Shauna, a pastor in Colorado, told me, "The best thing that happened to me was getting the s*** beat out of me at my last church." When we are able to get to this scary-yet-freeing reality of admitting we are high maintenance—where we are freely and regularly able to pray prayers of desperation, where we are able to see our failures as a gateway to a deepened relationship with the Father—we are then able to believe deep to our core that we truly are blessed. Ministry in its deepest sense rests in the belief that we make our wounds, scars and failures accessible to others as a source of healing, including our own. It's what makes Alcoholics Anonymous such an enduring movement of hope for so many.

Spiritual Wabi-Sabi

Accepting our brokenness as the foundation of true spiritual breakthrough reminds me of *wabi-sabi*, the Japanese form of art that finds its beauty in its purposeful imperfection. This type of art is seen as beautiful because it is imperfect and broken. It's the Japanese equivalent of broken stained glass. Characteristics of *wabi-sabi* are irregularity, roughness, brokenness and asymmetry. This art form acknowledges three simple but profound realities: nothing lasts, nothing is finished and nothing is perfect.[1] It perfectly communicates perfect imperfection.

According to Japanese legend, a young man named Sen no Rikyū sought to learn the elaborate set of customs known as the "Way of Tea." He went to tea master Takeno Jōō, who tested the younger man by asking him to tend the garden. Rikyū cleaned up debris and raked the ground until it was perfect and the garden immaculate. Before presenting his work to the master, he shook a cherry tree, causing a few flowers to fall onto the ground. To this day, the Japanese revere Rikyū as one who understood to his very core *wabi-sabi*. Emerging in the fifteenth century as a reaction to the prevailing aesthetic of lavishness, ornamentation and rich materials, *wabi-sabi* is the art of finding beauty in imperfection and profundity in earthiness, of revering authenticity above all.[2]

When a white pottery bowl breaks, for example, we might glue it back together with white lacquer to disguise the breaks, making it look as new and complete as possible. In the East the white pottery bowl might be glued back together with lacquer sprinkled with gold to highlight the cracks and imperfections. Japanese culture sees the aesthetic value of imperfection in *wabi-sabi* just as much as the Greeks valued perfection in their art. The gospel is spiritual *wabi-sabi*. To understand *wabi-sabi* is to grasp God's hallowing of hollowed-out, broken people to bless a harried world.[3] When we are weak, he is strong.

The Old Testament prophet Isaiah wrote, "by his wounds we are healed" (Is 53:5). If his wounds have healed us, we are carriers of extravagant hope. We become wounded healers through Christ. We serve the world most faithfully out of our pain and brokenness, not our strength and accolades; brokenness and authenticity honor God and inspire people.

Chronos and Kairos

There are two words in Greek for time—*chronos* and *kairos*. Chronos (where we get our word *chronology*) describes a very specific measurement of time—a sequence of events—for example, 3:45 on a Tuesday afternoon. But kairos time is different. It describes the more qualitative reality of time. If chronos deals with clocks and calendars, kairos deals with moments and seasons. It is time pregnant with possibility. Lawrence Cunningham describes kairos as "those moments, which are decisive, which open up the opportunity for conversion or commitment. . . . The kairos moment happens each time God's invitation in Christ is presented to us."[4]

Kairos time is rarely neutral; it leaves a mark on our lives, either positive or negative. These times remain in our heads and hearts as some of our deepest, most lasting memories. Our lives are measured by chronos time, but they are marked by kairos time—and each one demands a response from us. More often than not, the biblical writers were describing time in the reality of kairos, not chronos; they were much more concerned with timing than with time.[5] It's no wonder the biblical writers used *kairos* almost twice as much as *chronos*. But is easy to focus so much of our attention on chronos minutes that we miss kairos moments.

It has been said that God gets our attention most effectively through beauty and suffering: both are poignant kairos moments. Failure is always a kairos moment. It implies some sort of suffering. You will never experience a significant failure in your life that is not a kairos moment. Failure is a crucible experience; it is a call, a challenge and a test. Failure is a terrible thing to waste. How will we respond to kairos moments in chronos time?

Our failures have a way of reminding us that not only are we a part of the broken human race but also that God can use us in our failings rather than disqualify us from our callings. Mature leaders, who have experienced deep, indelible brokenness do not feel the pressure to perpetually strive for the approval of others or have a deep-seated need to impress those around them. A pastor who has been broken already knows what shame is, therefore there is little worry of being found out or seen as a failure. We already know that to be true.[6]

Thus many experienced pastors refuse to bring other pastors on their staff who have not been deeply wounded. They are convinced that a severely wounded pastor who has experienced a marking kairos moment and who has come to the place of acceptance rooted deeply in Christ is capable of pastoring other people well. Wounds do not eliminate them from ministry; instead, wounds educate, mature and prepare. In many ways failure, suffering and pain are the prerequisite for effective ministry. They strip away the false self and help us encounter the true self. They are part of the curriculum of life and ministry in a fallen world.

Shedding Our Dragon Skin

Failure is painful, but sometimes healing can be even more painful. C. S. Lewis's story *The Voyage of the Dawn Treader* gives us a glimpse into the pain of healing. A young, stubborn and selfish boy named Eustace finds himself on an island. As it begins to rain, Eustace seeks shelter in a cave and falls asleep. When he wakes up he feels strange and realizes he has turned into a dragon. He is scared and wants to turn back into a boy. One evening Eustace hears Aslan's voice calling out to him saying, "Follow me." Though as a dragon he could have eaten any lion, he is still afraid. Following Aslan, he finds himself by a pool where he wishes to wash his wounded leg, but Aslan tells him he must first undress. Using his dragon claws, he desperately scratches and claws himself to shed his dragon skin much like a snake sheds its skin. Three times he claws and scrapes in desperation, but each time he notices another layer of hard, rough scales. He realizes he is incapable of fully ridding himself of his scaly skin.

"You will have to let me undress you," Aslan tells him. Eustace recalls,

I was afraid of his claws, I can tell you, but I was pretty nearly desperate now. So I just lay flat down on my back and let him do it. The very first tear he made was so deep that I thought it had gone right into my heart. And when he began pulling the skin off, it hurt worse than anything I've ever felt. . . . Well, he peels the beastly stuff right off— just as I thought I'd done it myself the other three times, only they hadn't hurt—and there it was lying on the grass: only ever so much thicker, and darker, and more knobby looking than the others had been. And there was I as smooth and soft as a peeled switch. . . . Then he caught hold of me

. . . and threw me into the water. It smarted like anything but only for a moment. After that it became perfectly delicious and as soon as I started swimming and splashing I found that all the pain had gone from my arm. And then I saw why. I'd turned into a boy again.[7]

In the kingdom of God, dying is followed by resurrection. We cannot work through our failures on our own. Christ must undress us. Despite incredible pain, we find we are human again. It is only in our willingness to let Christ undragon us that we find true healing. But many of us are convinced it is better to remain a dragon, because it allows us to retain tough skin that will keep us from getting hurt again.

But as we explored earlier, if we numb the pain, we numb everything. When we do this, we become less human. Being a full-time pastor but a part-time human is one of the most dangerous paths a pastor can travel. It is one of the surest ways to failure: the failure to be a person first before being a pastor.[8] The good but costly news of Jesus is the invitation to be humans, not dragons.

We need others to remind us of the truth. Sometimes it is the subtle but clear promptings from the Spirit. It may come in the form of a passage of Scripture that grabs us by the throat or comforts us to the point of tears. Other times it may come in gentle encouragement or the direct rebuke from a trusted friend. All these are gracious gifts from God.

Bringing Our Nothing

We are often the older brother in the parable of the prodigal son. We are driven by duty, motivated by loyalty and measured by responsibility. For many of us perfectionism and performance are hardwired in our DNA. If left unchecked, this veiled and self-righteous pride whispers, *Just look at what I've done for you, God.*

For years I thought the parable was wrongly named. I thought it should be called the parable of the prodigal sons. It wasn't until I understood prodigal meant "squanderer" or "one who wastes significantly" that I grasped that it is the parable of the prodigal son—I had been focusing on the wrong son. When I worry about being morally dutiful and spiritually responsible, I miss the point, squandering the love the Father has been offering to me the entire time I've lived under his roof.

Receiving can be difficult, especially for pastors whose job is to provide care for others. Why do we grimace at the thought of having others wash our feet? Why do we prefer the position of washing to being washed? Often, identity can easily be wrapped up in the fact that we are providers and servants. When we receive the gift of having our feet washed by others, we are admitting we cannot do this on our own; we need others. There may be no set of leaders that struggles with others washing their feet more than those in ministry.

The most vulnerable thing we could ever do, the thing that requires the most courage and faith, is the key to freedom. We *bring our nothing*—accepting who we are by accepting who God is, what he has done and what he promises to do. Again, we know this. We preach this. But this doesn't always get into our bloodstream.

When failure hits we may be tempted to try to pull ourselves up by our bootstraps and try harder next time. The *just try harder* mentality, wrapped in the cloak of American self-sufficiency and spiritual professionalism, sets us back into the unending cycle. It is not the cycle of godlessness that most often destroys pastors but the cycle of religiosity.

Religiosity is what Dallas Willard calls the "Gospel of Sin Management."[9] When we truly come to a place of freedom, we are not gripping harder on the problem but are releasing it. This is not apathetic resignation but an active letting go. It is a faith-filled letting go of our attempt to do it ourselves. When we let go of trying to control ourselves, we can also let go of attempting to control the people in our churches. Pastor, here's tremendously freeing good news: you are not God's answer to every problem or situation in your church—despite what others, including the people in your church, may tell you.

Learning to Hug the Cactus

Earlier I shared my story of deep hurt and pain that I am still recovering from. Despite the heartache, there is a thread of redemption that is so beautiful it validates the scars. The first sermon I preached at our old church was a part of a series called "Wounds That Time Doesn't Heal." My sermon topic was betrayal. I preached on the life of Jeremiah and his harsh words when he calls God a liar, shaking his fist and yelling to the skies "You deceived me, LORD, and I was deceived."

At the end of the sermon I shared how Megan and I had felt what Jeremiah had felt through the recent news of our infertility. As I preached and shared, a middle-aged couple who attended the second service also felt betrayed, but in a different way. They had recently found out their daughter, away at college, was pregnant. They were at a loss: how could they parent well in the midst of the shocking news and relational tension? After the service they drove home in silence. When they pulled in their driveway, they looked at each other and asked, "Are you thinking what I'm thinking?" With a nod of agreement, they contacted the church that week, asking if they could meet with Megan and me. It was the first time we met the birth family of our oldest son, Carter.

God had connected relational dots and introduced us to a family who paved the way for Megan and me to experience parenthood through the miracle of adoption. It was a redemption story we never could have imagined. It was literally the most life-altering sermon I've ever preached. God has a way of redeeming stories—even when the key players in the story are heartbroken and confused.

Despite the searing pain, had we never experienced infertility we never would have met Carter, who is now almost seven years old. God's grace has been abundant in placing him into our home—along with our other adopted son, Bennett. Had we been able to have our own biological children, we never would have met our two boys—a thought we cannot fully fathom. We have come to rally around a phrase used by theologian Miroslav Volf— the father of two adopted boys—"the gift of infertility."[10]

We were finally able to "hug the cactus"—to come to accept and embrace our weaknesses, limitations and brokenness as a vital part of our healing and growth.[11] God has given us the two greatest gifts in our marriage through the most devastating pain we have endured. Looking back, we were able to see God had not deceived us after all. Despite the hurt and the wounds of our previous church experience, we would do it again just to meet our son. If the only reason we went through the dark years was to enter into parenthood, we embrace that. God's redemptive work does not erase the bad tapes in my mind and heart. They are still there and get replayed from time to time, but they remind me of the redemptive purposes behind the bad tapes. We have been so blessed. God's invitation of grace will never make sense to me. It's too wild and expansive.

Paul's words, in fresh language, reveal the heart of accepting failure:

> He said to me, "My grace is enough for you. When you are weak, my power is made perfect in you." So I am very

happy to brag about my weaknesses. Then Christ's power can live in me. For this reason I am happy when I have weaknesses, insults, hard times, sufferings, and all kinds of troubles for Christ. Because when I am weak, then I am truly strong. (2 Cor 12:9-10 NCV)

Paul hugs the cactus. "So I am very happy to brag about my weaknesses." That is a man who found the cross to be a ladder rescuing him out of the pity of his own sin and limitations. That is a man who found acceptance in his failure because he found his identity in the gospel. There is no spiritual formation and maturity without difficulty and uncertainty. If we are going to continue to grow in our journey with Jesus, we have to continue to risk, opening ourselves up to the possibility of failing again. God, the great failure redeemer, is the only one who can undragon us in order to be human again.

11

RHYTHMS

Restorative Practices for the Way Forward

*Just as we have an overflowing share of the
Messiah's sufferings, you see, so we have
an overflowing share in comfort
through the Messiah.*

**2 Corinthians 1:5
(New Testament for Everyone)**

*What does the world need: gifted men and women
outwardly empowered? Or individuals who
are broken, inwardly transformed?*

Gene Edwards, *A Tale of Three Kings*

Learning the Unforced Rhythms of Grace

After singing a few worship songs, we were just about to end the
first evening of one of our Epic Fail Pastors events when I saw a
hand in the back. A young church planter was so burned out he
looked crispy around the edges. He leaned back in his chair and

said, "This may be way off topic, but we sing these songs about Jesus and I don't even know who Jesus is anymore or what I believe about him."

He paused. "Can someone tell me the gospel again? I need to hear it." After a long silence a pastor across the room cleared his throat and shared the outlandishly good news of the life, death and resurrection of Jesus. When the pastor was finished speaking, the church planter looked up, smiled and said, "Thanks. I needed that."

It was a sacred moment—and it most certainly was not off topic. In fact, it might have been the most significant three minutes of the entire event. As pastors, maybe more than almost anybody else, we need to preach the gospel to ourselves or at least have the courage to ask others to preach it to us.

Jesus spoke healing words to the tired and worn out, even those who serve and lead in the church.

Are you tired? Worn out? Burned out on religion? Come to me. Get away with me and you'll recover your life. I'll show you how to take a real rest. Walk with me and work with me—watch how I do it. Learn the unforced rhythms of grace. I won't lay anything heavy or ill-fitting on you. Keep company with me and you'll learn to live freely and lightly. (Mt 11:28-30 *The Message*)

Jesus was not just writing fortune-cookie sayings; he is offering us life of the highest and purest measure. It is an invitation dripping with hope. Each word in the passage carries rich meaning. My favorite phrase (which I have quoted dozens of times to burdened pastors) is *learn the unforced rhythms of grace.*

Learn. This phrase puts pastors in the role of students, seeking to learn from the master Teacher what right living—and light living—look like.

Unforced. In a world—and a calling—that seems to force itself on us, dictating what we should and should not do, we are called into a life that is unforced. An unforced life is beautiful to watch. Bring force into the mix and it breeds legalism and an awkward and unnatural way of life. When a dance is forced, it is difficult to watch; when it is unforced, it is beautifully graceful. Life with God is a dance.

Rhythms. Rhythm brings consistency and stability but it is not rote. Rhythms are not ruts; they are practices saturated in life and liveliness. Because rhythms anchor us, we can live with texture, depth and spontaneity.

Grace. The engine of the gospel runs on the fuel of grace. Life-giving rhythms rooted in grace are beautiful. It is impossible to have forced rhythms of grace; grace is always unforced.

How can I learn such a thing from Jesus? "Keep company with me, and you'll learn to live lightly and freely." Even though Jesus is inviting me in on the most relational of expressions, I still struggle to grasp it.

How do we move forward with equal measures of reality and hope? I want to be ridiculously practical by offering potential next steps. These restorative practices have helped pastors—including me—rehab their souls. The goal is to offer practices that help us get up off the canvas and keep moving, even if all we can do is limp or crawl.

These are not required items on a spiritual to-do list; they are merely suggestions. Doing all of them is probably unrealistic and potentially exhausting. View them as encouragement on the path of recovery, wholeness and healing. Consider choosing two or three that may be helpful for you, but attempting to incorporate all of them into your life may set yourself up for more failure.

The Need to Breathe

FAA regulations require flight attendants to communicate specific safety instructions before any commercial flight in North America. They include:

Should the cabin lose pressure, oxygen masks will fall from the ceiling panels above your head. Pull the mask toward you, placing it over your nose and mouth. Tighten the straps and breathe normally. If traveling with small children or those in need of assistance, please secure your mask before assisting others.

Initially, such actions might seem selfish. Why tighten your straps first? In a time of emergency, shouldn't we be thinking of others? It is, however, incredibly strategic: if I am breathing appropriately, I can help not just myself but others around me. If I am unable to breathe, I cannot help others or myself.

How often are we tempted to believe that in times of crisis we can help others without breathing in the breath of the Spirit ourselves? I can operate without oxygen for a little while, but ultimately it will catch up with me. It is not selfish to adjust my mask and tighten the straps around my soul first. We are called to lead others, but our ministry comes out of the overflow of our own lives. We must learn to gain the urgency for soul care and acknowledge the lie that taking care of ourselves is selfish. We need to learn to breathe.

Peter Scazzero writes about how we make excuses about the other ("nonspiritual") areas of our lives. It is easy to deprioritize our physical life (*Who has time to exercise or eat right or to get enough rest?*), our social life (*Don't worry about those friendships. Who has time for healthy relationships and significant others?*), our intellectual life (*Be wary of developing your mind to its full potential. You'll end up with no heart for God. Who has time for reflection anyway?*) and our emotional life (*It seems that when you get in touch with your feelings, you become more confused and not close to God*).[1] We cannot ignore these areas of our lives, for each one has vast implications for our souls. They matter in how we lead, live and love. Self-care is the first step in caring for others, for loving your neighbor as *yourself*. I offer these suggestions as a way to tighten the straps of the oxygen mask around our souls so we can learn the unforced rhythms of grace.

Relationships and Support

Secure a mentor, coach or spiritual director. As mentioned in chapters eight and nine, research reveals that one of the most significant tools for failure recovery is securing a coach or a spiritual director. Having someone walk alongside you in your recovery is crucial to healing. Both a life coach and a spiritual director are helpful, but which one would be most helpful for you may depend on personality, spiritual temperament or what the season of life or ministry is requiring of you.[2]

Attend a small group you do not lead. We need to be in healthy community with other believers, but without the responsibility of leadership. Find a smaller grouping of people that meets regularly where you and your spouse can be regular people. Pastors need to find places where they can be honest. This group may best be found outside of the context of your church or former church.

Find a trusted Christian counselor. My only regret with seeing a Christian counselor was that I did not go sooner—and more often. If there is any pride keeping you from going to see a counselor, my word to you is: Get over yourself. You are a broken sinner in need of grace. Even if you sense everything is fine in this season of life and ministry, I still encourage you to see a counselor. Why wait until there is a major problem? We take our cars in for tune-ups and our bodies in for physicals and checkups.

Why would we not take our hearts in for a checkup too? Allow a counselor to pop the hood of your heart and poke around. You may be surprised with what he or she finds. A wise Christ-centered counselor can be valuable in reminding us that ministry may demand our time but cannot define our identity.

Yes, counseling can be expensive, but it can be significant in your healing. Seek out ways to have the cost covered. Consider adjusting your budget to make it work. If appropriate, consider approaching the leadership of the church to see if the church would cover the counseling costs for you and your spouse. Certain kinds of counseling are covered on medical plans or are reimbursable using a medical flex plan account. If that is not an option, approach a few trusted friends and ask if they might help cover costs. Whatever you do, make sure money isn't the primary reason you don't think seriously about counseling.

Connect regularly with other pastors. Are there other pastors you have met who you sense are safe to process grief and thoughts of failure? Consider connecting with them monthly over coffee or lunch. They can become your partners as together you limp along the path of healing and grace. We need people who inherently understand the joys and wounds of ministry; meeting regularly can remind us we are not alone.

Develop friends who don't need you. Developing friendships that see you as a person first and as pastor second (or third, fourth or fifth) is essential to wholehearted living. Interactions may not always include deep conversations about life's most significant issues. Your time together may include watching movies, drinking good wine, going to a ballgame or shooting hoops. Here our emotional, relational and mental buckets are replenished.

Develop a prayer team with whom you can vent and be truly honest. Create a team of wise, trusted, godly people who will not merely pray for you but commit to prayer and intercession on your behalf. This sort of prayer team is like the four anonymous friends in Mark 2. They carried their paralyzed friend and started digging a hole in the roof of a house so he could be lowered down to Jesus. What would it look like if you had friends who dug holes in roofs on your behalf to get you to feet of Jesus?

Recalibration and Realignment

Give up reading how-to ministry books. In appropriate seasons and spaces, how-to resources can be helpful in developing skills and learning from others. However, if left unchecked, they can lead to reinforced feelings of insecurity and even idolatry. Most of the surefire strategies shared in those books are highly contextualized; it may work in the author's ministry setting, but in yours it may feel forced and unnatural. Avoid them—especially the ones that smell like fads or play to fast-changing ministry trends. Instead, invest your time reading theology, church history or biographies of faithful pastors and leaders.

Consider reading Eugene Peterson and Henri Nouwen. Peterson, who pastored almost as long as I have been alive, has written several books on pastoral vocation. I recommend *The Unnecessary Pastor* (cowritten with Marva Dawn), *The Pastor, Five Smooth Stones for Pastoral Work, Under the Unpredictable Plant* and *The Contemplative Pastor.*

Nouwen writes with a mystical style that turns our attention to the loving heart of God. His book *In the Name of Jesus* is one of the best and most insightful books on Christian leadership of the past few decades. It is worth its weight in gold.

I would also add David Hansen's *The Art of Pastoring: Ministry Without All the Answers.* This is a refreshing look at what countercultural yet faithful ministry to Jesus can look like. There are many others worth mentioning. If you desire to go further in your reading and reflection, a list of recommended books is included in appendix one.

Also consider picking up nonministry and non-Christian books. Read a classic novel that you never had time for, or something entirely different than the norm, but a topic you're interested in.

Journal—and be raw, blunt and honest if needed. If you try journaling as a spiritual practice, let me provide a few questions to help prompt some thought and reflection:

- Read Ecclesiastes 3:1-8 and ask, What season am I in currently?

- What opportunities and limitations exist in this season of life?

- What are the top one or two dominating emotions I'm feeling this week or month. And what might that reveal God wants to change in me?[3]

- What do I need right now and am I humble and courageous enough to ask for help from those who care about my well-being?

- Where is God meeting me in this season of my life? Where would I like God to meet me in this season of life? When will I tell him?

- What words over the past week or month have carried the most meaning for me?

- What do I feel when I feel emotionally exposed? Why?

- How do I behave when I'm feeling very uncomfortable and uncertain?

- How willing am I to take emotional risks right now?

- How—and in what areas—is my fear of vulnerability holding me back?[4]

Talk with your church leaders about what success and failure look like. Frustration is the difference between expectation and reality; the larger the gap, the more the frustration. How often our frustration is rooted in inaccurate assumptions. It takes courage to enter into conversation with church leadership and maybe even the entire congregation as to what we are after in our ministry.

Many pastors have told me they are not sure what is expected of them. This has led to a significant amount of insecurity, anxiety and sleeplessness. Talking about proper expectations may be difficult, but in the long run can be incredibly healthy and comforting. See appendix two for several guiding questions that may help you to develop a clear purpose with your leaders.

Watch Brené Brown's TED videos. Consider watching and processing Brené Brown's two eighteen-minute TED Talk videos[5] with your staff, elders or leaders. Discuss the similarities and differences to the Christian experience and where you resonated the most with her thoughts.

Talk it out. Cry. Weep. Yell. Letting out our emotions can be incredibly therapeutic. In *Praying the Psalms* Thomas Merton wrote that one of the best ways to come to appreciate the psalms is to develop the habit of reading then aloud slowly and considerately.[6] Soak in the waters of the psalms until your soul looks like prunes. Consider writing your own psalms, in your own language, addressing your own situation and emotions, even if they aren't pretty.

One pastor told me his therapy costs him $7 a session—the cost of a large bucket of golf balls at the driving range. Another told me he had once gone to the thrift store and bought a box of old glassware, went to his basement when his family members were not home and threw each piece of glassware against the wall as hard as he could. He was more honest is his prayers and felt closer to God during those broken dish moments than any time since becoming a pastor.

As he cleaned up the mess, he cried, thanking God for the healing he had experienced in letting out his emotions all at once. You may not want to try something so severe or intense. The point is that grieving is a normal part of the human experience—and God can meet us in the most intense expressions of our grief. The worst thing we can we do is bury it. Let it out when appropriate, even if it is intense.

Avoid conferences that promote Christian celebrities and events that highlight ministry success. In dark seasons of failure, avoid attending pastors' conferences that promote the celebrity pastors who are on multicity speaking tours. I am certain they are good men and women, but it is the unmentioned value statements that speak the loudest and clearest at these events. It can fuel unhealthy thoughts and ambitions in our hearts and minds. There may be a season to reenter these spaces; if so, it might be wise to attend with other trusted and grounded conversation partners who can dialogue with you during and after the event.

Model the go-first principle. We are called to model what life in the kingdom looks like. In the kingdom, weakness is power, loss is gain, dying is actually the beginning of living and death leads to resurrection. When we are healthy and lead out of our failure and brokenness we give others a gift. If our preaching gives our church the impression we have it all together, then we are doing it all wrong. People are waiting for permission to speak honestly and courageously about their brokenness; that permission is granted when they see it done by the person up front. Go first.

It will be excruciating at times, but go first. Going first may mean not only confessing to others but also forgiving others. One pastor told me, "I know I'm supposed to forgive, but I don't want to do it. If I don't forgive them I have power over them, and I don't want to give up that power." Forgiving others first can be agonizing, especially when people may not ask for forgiveness or believe they weren't wrong at all. The Spanish poet Antonio

Machado wrote, "Traveler, there is no path, the path must be forged as you walk." It starts with us.

Rediscovering Rest and Joy

Practice sabbath. I have yet to meet a burned-out pastor who practiced sabbath religiously. Sabbath is God's clearest invitation to "learn the unforced rhythms of grace." It is a day to pray and play. Instead of rest from work, we must enter into a new mindset where we work from rest.

As a driven, people-pleasing, extroverted, recovering perfectionist, I'm certain I would have been a burned-out statistic by now if I did not practice sabbath. It is the day I am forced to trust God most, as it confronts my deepest pride and my longing for progress and efficiency. If you are the head of your church, then you better get busy because there is too much for you to do. But if Christ is the head of your church, then you need to slow down and listen to what he desires. Sabbath is not only a day of deep rest; it is also a day of deep trust.

Peter Scazzero writes that sabbath is like God giving his people a big snow day once a week.[7] It is a weekly reminder that our identity is not wrapped up in what we do but in who we are—and more importantly to whom we belong.

God is the head of the church. This includes the local expression of it he has entrusted to you to serve and lead. He is not worried about how the church will manage if you take a day to slow down, be present and rest. Your church will not unravel because you take one day every week to rest. However, if you refuse to rest, chances are eventually you might be the one unraveling.

Participate in life-giving activities. We can easily disregard life-giving activities because they seem trivial. Shouldn't we be focusing on the most eternally significant matters? It is more important for leaders to focus on energy management than time management. When the tank is low, where do you go to fill it up? Certainly, the Lord is our source and our strength, but God also offers us the gift of restoration in the form of activities, hobbies and life-giving experiences. These might include hunting or photography, playing chess or quilting, spending a Saturday afternoon in a canoe or curling up on the couch, running a half-marathon or reading a good novel.

In my office near the window is a large gumball machine. It was a going away present from the leadership team of my church in Colorado. The leaders had heard me ask dozens of times, "How's your gumball machine?" It was a soul care question. They knew the story well: the first time I visited a Christian counselor and shared how empty I felt and how emotionally, physically and spiritually exhausted I was, he drew me a picture. It was a poor drawing of a gumball machine. *I paid you $100 to have you draw me a bad picture of a gumball machine?* I thought. *This is ridiculous.* He explained it seemed my gumball machine was empty—or close to it. It was important to make sure I had gumballs in the machine or the people I was leading would grow increasingly frustrated with me—just like how people react when they put a quarter into the machine and nothing comes out.

He told me I had one of three options if I was going to be healthy again. Unscrew the top of the machine and ask God's Spirit to pour new gumballs of life into me in order to fill me up again. Tape an "Out of Order" sign to the front of the machine until I had recovered. Or both. He handed me the sheet of paper and said, "It sounds like it would be wise to list some life-giving activities to participate in. It would do your soul a lot of good to see some gumball-increasing activities integrated into your life."

I look back on that session as one of the most important practical pieces of wise, godly counsel I have received in ministry. It is amazing how life-giving activities can lead us to experiencing a full heart, one that seeks to be filled in order to pour out to others. Even running, quilting, canoeing or playing chess can be a beautiful act of worship to God.

What activities—simply for your enjoyment and pleasure—might you add to your schedule?

Get out of the ZIP Code. Every few months my soul is in need of a day outside of the ZIP Code. Geographical distance from my primary context helps me regain perspective. Getting out of my ZIP Code gives me perspective on the mural of ministry and allows me to see the whole picture for what it is. I slow down, breathe deeper and feel freer—even if I am just ten miles away from home. I look forward to these days to slow down, pay attention and be with God—regardless of how he chooses to interact with me.

Exercise and eat well. Pastors as a whole are terrible at self-care. One study found that nutrition, physical exercise and other forms of self-care were lower priorities for pastors than for the general population.[8] Age for age, clergy have significantly greater incidences of chronic disease, heart and GI tract conditions and stress. Clergy today have significantly worse health than the average American.[9]

First Kings 17–19 records the dramatic ministry experiences of Elijah. He was exhausted and suicidal. Though he saw God's glory poured out, Elijah wanted to die. The exhaustion, the crises and the loneliness caught up to him. What he needed came in two seemingly nonspiritual forms: sleep and food.

He lay down under a broom tree and slept. An angel touched him and told him to get up, eat a hot cake and drink a jar of water. He fell asleep again. An angel woke him up again and told him to eat. Sleep. Eat. Sleep. Eat. It was God's way of handing Elijah the oxygen mask and encouraging him to pull the straps tightly around his face. Then God showed up—not through wind or earthquake or fire, but through a low whisper.[10] Elijah encountered God afresh through a process—and a significant part of the process included scandalously ordinary activities: Naps. Hot cakes. A jar of water. And silence.

Our bodies are intricately connected to our souls. Joining a health club or gym and healthy eating can impact your body and your soul in recovery. These changes and others like them may be more significant than you think. Maybe the most spiritual thing you do this week is take a nap or go for a jog.

Take a moment to reflect on these restorative practices. Which ones might be worth implementing in order to help you heal? And who might walk alongside of you? Restorative practices can take us by the hand and lead us down the path to healing. May you hear Jesus' clear invitation to keep company with him as you learn the unforced rhythms of grace.

A DIFFERENT F-WORD

The Beautiful Mess of Freedom

I have told you these things, so that in me
you may have peace. In this world you
will have trouble. But take heart!
I have overcome the world.

John 16:33

All ministry begins at the ragged
edges of our own pain.

Ian Morgan Cron,
Chasing Francis

Even the Beggars Are Invited

Martin Luther's last words before he died on February 18, 1546, were written on a scrap of paper: "We are beggars. This is true."

We celebrate the Lord's Supper as beggars. Jesus breaks his body and he pours out his blood for a broken world so we might be whole again. *Eucharist* means "the great thanksgiving"—for it is our saving hope as failed beggars. The Communion table invites beggars to come empty and leave full.

The voluntary admission of our failure—the confession of sin—is the threshold to the home of forgiveness. It is the entrance exam to life in the kingdom and the key that opens the door to a restored relationship with God. The very basis of our calling in ministry is predicated on the admission of our failure. Embracing our brokenness is the only path to freedom. We may be stumbling friends of Jesus, but we are friends, no less.

Satan is half-right: We are failures. We are broken. We are sinful. The evil one will do his best to keep us locked in to only half of the truth. But the cross refuses to leave us there. It carries us to the second half of the truth: God is love. Jesus is enough. We are forgiven. We are invited into healing in order to experience redemption. We are invited into a life of wholeness and freedom. The life, death and resurrection of Jesus change the F-word from the sadness of *failure* to the challenge of *faithfulness* to the hope of *freedom*.

The Communion elements remind us that failure is not the end of the story. Jesus ends up eating with all sorts of "wrong" people. Is it any surprise, then, that he invites failed beggars like us to pull up a chair and raise a glass? The outlandish love of God is so large, so great, so wide and so encompassing that it seems scandalous. It is the beautiful mess of freedom.

Dallas Willard, in his classic work *The Divine Conspiracy*, gives us a striking picture of the depth of the love and grace of our heavenly Father:

> The flunk-outs and drop-outs and burned-outs. The broke and the broken. The drug heads and the divorced. The HIV-positive and herpes-ridden. The brain-damaged, the incurably ill. The barren and the pregnant too many times or

at the wrong time. The over-employed, the underemployed, the unemployed. The unemployable. The swindled, the shoved aside, the replaced. The parents with children living on the street, the children with parents not dying in the "rest" home. The lonely, the incompetent, the stupid. The emotionally starved or emotionally dead. And on and on and on. . . . Jesus offers to all such people as these the present blessedness of the present kingdom—regardless of circumstances. . . . Murderers and child-molesters. The brutal and the bigoted. Drug lords and pornographers. War criminals and sadists. Terrorists. The perverted and the filthy and the filthy rich. . . .

Can't we feel some sympathy for Jesus' contemporaries, who huffed at him, "This man is cordial to sinners, and even eats with them!" Sometimes I feel I don't really want the kingdom to be open to such people. But it is. That is the heart of God. . . .

If I, as a recovering sinner myself, accept Jesus' good news, I can go to the mass murderer and say, "You can be blessed in the kingdom of the heavens. There is forgiveness that knows no limits." To the pederast and the perpetrator of incest. To the worshiper of Satan. To those who rob the aged and weak. To the cheat and the liar, the bloodsucker and the vengeful: Blessed! Blessed! Blessed! As they flee into the arms of The Kingdom Among Us.[1]

When this gospel hits me with strong force and deep hope, I cannot ignore its power—nor can I simply preach it to others without it messing with me first. The manna he gives for us while we wander in the wilderness is his broken body. This type of bread is our only shot at freedom. We are beggars. This is true.

When God Kisses Your Bruises

I wrote in the beginning of the book about my insecurity because I was not ordained. After having written the majority of this book, I received overwhelming news. Of course, everyone's journey is different, and we are all in different places. I certainly don't intend to communicate that everyone's story of pain will wrap up nicely in a pretty bow, but God gave me a gift I will never forget.

At the end of one of our elder meetings, the elders turned to me and said it was time. Not knowing the depth of my internal struggle about ordination, they told me it was long overdue and should have been done long ago. My ordination service would be held in the next several weeks. A date had already been set. Friends, family, other pastors and those representing our church planting network had already made plans to attend and participate. In addition, our church was prepared to affirm something the elders said our church already knew. When they told me this, it was impossible to hold back all that was being unleashed in me. I wept uncontrollably. The elders surrounded me and prayed joyfully over me.

My ordination service in February was one of the most encouraging and affirming days of the past decade of my ministry. The worship, Scripture readings, stories, charge, Communion and prayers were healing salve for my soul. After the charge, my wife and sons were invited up. Our church family, out-of-town friends and pastors surrounded us, laid hands on us and prayed.

Years of hurt and pain began to be repaired in that moment. As people returned to their seats, one of our elders presented me to the congregation as Reverend J.R. Briggs. Our church stood to their feet and clapped, shouted, cheered, whistled and jumped up and down in celebration.

I wept harder—each tear a liquid prayer, thanking God for

this healing experience and for his call on my life, and that he used a broken man like me to join him in this life of ministry with such compassionate people. In a deep and real way, I felt the affirmation of God through the affirmation of friends, family and a loving church.

To end the service, Chris, a pastor from Maryland and one of my dearest friends, called forward my son Carter, who, unbeknownst to me, had written a prayer to close the service. Carter, with assistance from Chris, read his prayer: "Dear God, thank you that Daddy is a good pastor and that I know he loves you and will love you forever and ever. God, I pray that he would continue to be a good pastor. Amen."

It was a kiss from God on my bruises.

A Final Blessing

I end with a blessing from Larry Hine, Brennan Manning's spiritual director, who delivered this benediction at Manning's ordination service:

> May all of your expectations be frustrated,
> May all of your plans be thwarted,
> May all of your desires be withered into nothingness,
> That you may experience the powerlessness and poverty
> of a child, and can sing and dance in the love of
> God the Father, Son and Holy Spirit.
> Amen.

As you limp and stumble through failure, may it usher you to the place where one day you can sing and dance with Father, Son and Spirit.

ACKNOWLEDGMENTS

No book can be written without encouragement and support from others. When writing a book on failure, the need becomes even more essential.

Thanks to Dr. Derek Cooper. Without his perpetual nudges to put the ideas in my head and heart onto paper, this project might never have come to fruition.

Thanks to the Epic Fail Pastor Events planning team—Jason Sheffield, Michael Smith, Mandy Smith and Adam Gustine—who have worked tirelessly and faithfully to provide safe spaces for pastors to process the dangerous topics of failure and the gospel.

Thanks to Mandy Smith for her tireless work on the manuscript. I am inestimably grateful for her constant encouragement and insightful feedback throughout. Without her involvement this book would not be nearly what it has become.

Thanks to Dennis Brice, Alan Briggs, Tom Smith, Dave Briggs, Scott Kregel and Tracy Commons for reading early chapters of the manuscript and providing thorough and wise feedback along the way.

Thanks to Dr. Stephen Burrell for sharing his significant research on amoral ministry failure in chapters eight and nine. I'm so grateful you picked up the phone and called me.

Thanks to Scot McKnight, Skye Jethani, Eugene Peterson, Ruth Graham, John Julien and Jared Mackey, who have been encouraging conversation partners in the journey, helping me develop a more robust, clear and hope-filled theology of failure rooted in the extravagantly good news of Jesus.

Thanks to my agent, Andrew Wolgemuth, who believed in this idea—and in me—enough to take a risk on a project on failure. From Wengatz Hall to this. Who knew?

Thanks to my editor, Al Hsu, for his meticulous work and wise feedback in making this message as tight, clear and compelling as possible. His involvement was invaluable to the process.

Thanks to the engaging, professional and fun people at InterVarsity Press. I am incredibly proud to be working with such a gracious and thoughtful team.

Thanks to my assistant, Courtney Adams, who edited every page and made sure the writing process—and my life—were in order. Though it may be invisible to the reader, her fingerprints are on every page of this book.

Thanks to the hundreds of courageous pastors who have shared their stories of pain, wounds, heartache and redemption the past several years. Your courage inspires me and your brokenness keeps me on my knees.

Thanks to Doug Moister, the elders, leaders and compassionate people of The Renew Community, our spiritual family. Thank you for loving my family and me well. What a ride it's been. I am honored to serve as one of your pastors.

Thanks to my wife, Megan, and my sons, Carter and Bennett, for your continued patience and love for me, even when I have been wrecked by the stories of wounded and failed pastors. Thank you for the ongoing grace you've extended to me when you've been affected by my failures as a husband and dad. I'm so glad we're in this together.

And thanks to Jesus, who—in an expression of his outlandish compassion—continues to love me despite my failures.

REFLECTION QUESTIONS

Chapter 1: Failure

1. At the beginning of Epic Fail Pastors events two questions are asked of the pastors: Why are you here, and what are you feeling? As you think about your experience, why you are reading this book, and as you read it what are you feeling?

2. How does your relationship with failure affect how you view ministry? How does your relationship with ministry affect how you view failure?

3. Think about the failure-rejection-shame process. Can you identify yourself in that process when failure occurs? What is your default method in response to those situations?

4. Have you experienced the acceptance-honor process fueled by the gospel or are you stuck on the rejection-shame track? What would have to happen for you to experience acceptance and honor more often?

5. Think about the idea of freedom in Christ being *nothing to hide, nothing to lose and nothing to prove*. Is that realistic? Is it even possible? If so, when have you experienced this as a reality? What might that look like in your own life in the future? And how might that reality affect others?

Chapter 2: Success

1. What narratives of success play in your head and heart most regularly? What impact does that have on you?

2. How do you define success? Where was that metric derived? Who or what has spoken into that definition?

3. What metric of success does your church operate from, whether expressed, perceived or assumed? Is that encouraging or unsettling to you? What might happen if you operated out of a different metric?

4. In all truth and honesty, how would you feel if, for the rest of your life, God called you to pastor a church that never rose above forty people in average weekly attendance or involvement? How would that affect your thoughts about God?

5. Of the four types of failures—a mighty fall, a tragic event, a slow leak and a burned-out statistic—which best describes you and your ministry, or which do you most fear? Why? How might close friends and family answer this question for you?

6. Eugene Peterson and Marva Dawn write that pastors are unnecessary. How does that make you feel? How might that impact your identity?

Chapter 3: Faithfulness

1. *How many? How often? How much?* How regularly do these questions come to your mind in regards to your ministry or former ministry? What might this reveal about what needs to change?

2. How is success defined in your context? Who defines it? How do we know if that is a biblically grounded definition of success?

3. When are you most tempted to ask, "Are the vegetables ready yet?" Why?

4. How closely do you believe the desire and drive for success is related to the alarmingly high burnout rate for pastors?

5. Faithfulness is not often recognized and honored in our culture. What do you think is the root of that neglect?

Chapter 4: Shame

1. What resonates the most with you from this chapter? Why?

2. What have been some of the most significant shaming moments of your life? How have they influenced the way you interact with God and with others? What might this reveal that God may want to change in you?

3. Think back over the past two months. Can you identify moments—both significant and insignificant—when you have experienced the dichotomy of either innocence-guilt or honor-shame? How did that affect you?

4. What would happen to you, your family, your friendships and your ministry if you never again exposed yourself through vulnerability? What areas of your life are you holding back now—and from whom?

5. When are the whispers of shame (*I will be worthy when . . .* and *Who do you think you are?*) the loudest? What triggers them? Why?

6. If the gospel was running undiluted through your bloodstream, how would that change your response to your shame tapes?

Chapter 5: Loneliness

1. To what level do you experience loneliness in ministry? When do you feel it most intensely?

2. Do you agree with Henri Nouwen that pastors are the least confessing people in the church? Why or why not? Does it

have to be this way? What if pastors were the most confessing people in the church? How might that change communities of faith? How might that affect you?

3. When are you most tempted to reach for a mask? Why is
mask wearing so prevalent in the church, which was founded
on grace? How did we get to this place?

4. What masks mentioned in this chapter are most appealing or
easily accessible to you? What masks weren't mentioned?
Ultimately, what are you trying to control when you reach for
a mask?

5. What might it look like for you to take off your mask—and
keep it off? What would it cost you? Is it worth it?

6. What would have to happen for you to be appropriately vulnerable as a pastor? How can pastors grow to see our vulnerability as a gift for others?

Chapter 6: Wounds

1. "It seems God is much more concerned with the transformation going on inside us than the circumstances around us
in order to understand freedom." Why is this true? How does
that affect the way you view God's character?

2. When are you tempted to pray "nice" prayers, though they
may not be fully honest?

3. When was the last time your prayers were not "nice"? What
prompted such an intense and honest expression?

4. How might raw and honest prayers assist you to pray similarly in the midst of difficult times?

5. What permission do we have for raw and honest prayer in
our interaction with God? How would this kind of prayer
affect others' prayer lives?

Chapter 7: Wilderness

1. After reading this chapter, how might you view the wilderness differently than before?

2. Identify the times when God has taken you through the desert in "the roundabout way." Why does he take us on such a journey?

3. Why is the wilderness the mailing address of God's people? Why can't God teach us the lessons of the wilderness without having to experience the wilderness?

4. How might God's leading in the wilderness be an act of grace? Are there situations when that does not seem possible? If so, give some examples.

5. How has the wilderness been a teacher in your life and ministry?

6. How might your life be different if you never experienced—or never would experience—wilderness times?

Chapter 8: Recovery

1. What in this chapter rang true? What did you disagree with? Why?

2. Are you able to identify yourself in the descriptions of grief? If so, where are you currently in the process? What emotions does this bring to the surface?

3. How might your friends or family describe your process of grief?

4. What do you sense the Spirit might be speaking to you through what you just read? What is the appropriate response moving forward?

5. Who is—or who could be—walking with you through your recovery process?

Chapter 9: Reentry

1. What wisdom from other failed pastors struck you the most? Why?

2. What advice or encouragement might you give to other wounded or failed pastors?

3. What practices have you found most helpful to your own recovery?

4. Of the practices described in this chapter, which two or three are worthy of implementing in your life this week? Why these? Who might help you do that?

5. How might your prayers, longings and aspirations for recovery be shaped by what you read in this chapter?

Chapter 10: Acceptance

1. How might your life reflect a posture of *wabi-sabi*? What specifically might that look like? What sacrifices would have to be made?

2. Think over the past few years of your life. What are the most significant kairos moments? How did you respond to them?

3. Why is it easier for us to focus on chronos moments to the neglect of kairos moments?

4. What kairos moments are you currently experiencing? How are they marking you?

5. In light of the gospel, what cactus are you hugging—what is the discomfort you are leaning into in order to experience deeper intimacy with the Father?

6. What might the experience of being "undragoned" be like for you? Despite the pain, would it be worth it?

Chapter 11: Rhythms

1. Finish this sentence: The three adjectives I would use to describe the current state of my soul would be . . .

2. Slowly reread the words of Matthew 11:28-30 in *The Message*. What word or phrase strikes you most directly? Why? What might your life look like if you learned the "unforced rhythms of grace"?

3. Of the rhythms suggested in this chapter, which two or three might be most beneficial in helping you move in the direction of grace-fueled freedom and healing?

4. What might it mean for you to secure the oxygen mask and tighten the straps around your soul in this season of your life? How can we guard against these rhythms becoming formulaic models or legalistic equations?

5. Why is soul care difficult for many pastors? Is it difficult for you? How would your family answer this question for you?

6. Who can walk alongside you, encouraging and challenging you in the midst of these rhythms of grace?

Epilogue

1. As you think about this book, what thoughts or insights influenced you most? Why?

2. What do you sense the Spirit is prompting you to do with what you read?

3. Who might benefit from hearing what you've processed and learned?

4. How has this book changed your view of God, of grace and of his call on your life? How might you be a good steward of those insights?

5. What implications might that have on your family and close
   friendships? What implications might this have on your
   ministry—either past, present or future?

6. Now what?

APPENDIX 1

Recommended Resources

Books

The Pastor's Inner World

Anderson, Ray S. *Self-Care.* Eugene, OR: Wipf & Stock, 2010.

Baker, Howard. *Soul Keeping.* Colorado Springs: NavPress, 1998.

Barton, Ruth Haley. *Sacred Rhythms.* Downers Grove, IL: InterVarsity Press, 2007.

Benner, David. *Sacred Companions.* Downers Grove, IL: InterVarsity Press, 2006.

Brown, Brené. *Daring Greatly.* New York: Gotham, 2012.

———. *The Gifts of Imperfection.* Center City, MN: Hazelden, 2010.

Lee, Cameron, and Kurt Frederickson. *That Their Work Will Be a Joy: Understanding and Coping with the Challenges of Pastoral Ministry.* Eugene, OR: Wipf & Stock, 2012.

London, H. B., and Neil B. Wiseman. *Pastors at Greater Risk.* Ventura, CA: Regal, 2003.

———. *Pastors at Risk.* Wheaton, IL: Victor Books, 1993.

Manning, Brennan. *Abba's Child.* Colorado Springs: NavPress, 2002.

———. *The Ragamuffin Gospel.* Sisters, OR: Multnomah Books, 2005.

Nouwen, Henri J. M. *In the Name of Jesus.* New York: Crossroad, 1989.

———. *Life of the Beloved.* New York: Crossroad, 2002.

Oswald, Roy. *Clergy Self-Care.* Herndon, VA: Alban Institute Publishing, 1995.

Rohr, Richard, and Andreas Ebert. *The Enneagram: A Christian Perspective.* New York: Crossroad, 2001.

Scazzero, Peter. *Emotionally Healthy Spirituality*. Nashville: Thomas Nelson, 2011.

Smith, Mandy. *Making a Mess and Meeting God*. Cincinnati: Standard Publishing, 2010.

Thrall, Bill, Bruce McNicol, and John S. Lynch. *The Cure: What If God Isn't Who You Think He Is and Neither Are You?* Colorado Springs: NavPress, 2011.

Williams, Margery. *The Velveteen Rabbit*. New York: Doubleday, 1922.

Perspective on Ministry Success

Barton, Ruth Haley. *Strengthening the Soul of Your Leadership*. Downers Grove, IL: InterVarsity Press, 2008.

Dawn, Marva J., and Eugene H. Peterson. *The Unnecessary Pastor: Rediscovering the Call*. Grand Rapids. Eerdmans, 1999.

Ford, Lance. *Unleader*. Kansas City. Beacon Hill, 2012.

Hansen, David. *The Art of Pastoring*. Downers Grove, IL: InterVarsity Press, 2012.

Hughes, R. Kent, and Barbara Hughes. *Liberating Ministry from the Success Syndrome*. Wheaton, IL: Crossway, 2008.

Jethani, Skye. *With: Reimagining the Way You Relate to God*. Nashville: Thomas Nelson, 2011.

Manning, Brennan. *All Is Grace: A Ragamuffin Memoir*. Colorado Springs: David C. Cook, 2011.

McGee, Robert S. *The Search for Significance*. Nashville: Thomas Nelson, 2003.

McNeal, Reggie. *Missional Renaissance*. San Francisco: Jossey-Bass, 2009.

Peterson, Eugene H. *The Pastor*. New York: HarperOne, 2011.

———. *Under the Unpredictable Plant*. Grand Rapids: Eerdmans, 1994.

Purves, Andrew. *The Crucifixion of Ministry*. Downers Grove, IL: InterVarsity Press, 2007.

Roy, Steven C. *What God Thinks When We Fail*. Downers Grove, IL: InterVarsity Press, 2011.

Schnase, Robert. *Ambition in Ministry*. Nashville: Abingdon, 1993.

Tripp, Paul David. *Dangerous Calling*. Wheaton, IL: Crossway, 2012.

Wilson, Michael Todd, and Brad Hoffman. *Preventing Ministry Failure*. Downers Grove, IL: InterVarsity Press, 2007.

Processing Wounds/Grief

Allender, Dan B., and Tremper Longman. *The Cry of the Soul*. Colorado Springs: NavPress, 1999.

Chittister, Joan. *Scarred by Struggle, Transformed by Hope*. Grand Rapids: Eerdmans, 2005.

Edwards, Gene. *A Tale of Three Kings*. Wheaton, IL: Tyndale House, 1992.

John of the Cross. *Dark Night of the Soul*. Mineola, NY: Dover Publications, 2003.

Lewis, C. S. *A Grief Observed*. New York: HarperOne, 2009.

Nouwen, Henri J. M. *The Wounded Healer*. New York: Image, 1972.

Smedes, Lewis. *Shame and Grace*. New York: HarperOne, 2009.

Taylor, Barbara Brown. *Leaving Church*. New York: HarperOne, 2007.

Tchividjian, Tullian. *Glorious Ruin*. Colorado Springs: David C. Cook, 2012.

Willingham, Russell. *Relational Masks*. Downers Grove, IL: InterVarsity Press, 2004.

Wilson, Sandra D. *Released from Shame*. Downers Grove, IL: InterVarsity Press, 2002.

Winter, Richard. *When Life Goes Dark*. Downers Grove, IL: InterVarsity Press, 2012.

Leading Through Failure and Disappointment

Allender, Dan B. *Leading with a Limp*. Colorado Springs: WaterBrook, 2006.

Anonymous. *Embracing Obscurity*. Nashville: B & H Publishing, 2012.

Balda, Janis Bragan, and Wesley D. Balda. *Handbook for Battered Leaders*. Downers Grove, IL: InterVarsity Press, 2013.

Barton, Ruth Haley. *Strengthening the Soul of Your Leadership*. Downers Grove, IL: InterVarsity Press, 2008.

Cloud, Henry. *Necessary Endings*. San Francisco: HarperBusiness, 2011.

Graham, Ruth. *In Every Pew Sits a Broken Heart: Hope for the Hurting*. Grand Rapids: Zondervan, 2004.

Hart, Archibald D. *Healing Life's Hidden Addictions*. Ann Arbor, MI: Vine Books, 1990.

Heuertz, Christopher L. *Unexpected Gifts*. Howard Books, 2013.

Nouwen, Henri J. M. *The Wounded Healer*. New York: Image, 1972.

Rohrer, David. *The Sacred Wilderness of Pastoral Ministry*. Downers Grove, IL: InterVarsity Press, 2012.

Scazzero, Peter, and Warren Bird. *The Emotionally Healthy Church*. Grand Rapids: Zondervan, 2003.

Volf, Miroslav. *Exclusion and Embrace*. Nashville: Abingdon, 1996.

Resting and Sabbath Keeping

Cloud, Henry, and John Townsend. *Boundaries*. Grand Rapids: Zondervan, 1992.

Hansel, Tim. *When I Relax I Feel Guilty*. Elgin, IL: Chariot Family Publishing, 1979.

Hart, Archibald D. *Adrenaline and Stress*. Nashville: Thomas Nelson, 1995.

Heschel, Abraham Joshua. *The Sabbath*. New York: Farrar, Straus and Giroux, 2005.

Sine, Christine. *Sacred Rhythms*. Grand Rapids: Baker, 2003.

Sleeth, Matthew. *24/6*. Wheaton, IL: Tyndale House, 2012.

Wirzba, Norman. *Living the Sabbath*. Grand Rapids: Brazos, 2006.

Media

Brown, Brené. "The Power of Vulnerability." TED. *YouTube*. Accessed January 1, 2013. www.youtube.com/watch?v=iCvmsMzlF7o.

———. "Listening to Shame." TED. *YouTube*. Accessed January 1, 2013. www.youtube.com/watch?v=psN1DORYYV0.

Everybody's Fine. Directed by Kirk Jones. Miramax Films, 2009.

The Man Who Planted Trees. Directed by Frédéric Black. 1987. *YouTube*. Accessed January 1, 2013. www.youtube.com/watch?v=v_7yEPNUXsU.

Meet the Robinsons. Directed by Stephen J. Anderson. Walt Disney Pictures, 2007.

Vander Laan, Ray. *Walking with God in the Desert*. DVD. Grand Rapids: Zondervan, 2010.

APPENDIX 2

Guiding Questions for Pastors and Leaders

THERE IS WISDOM IN PROCESSING significant topics with other wise and trusted brothers and sisters. Below are guiding questions to help initiate discussion about ministry, failure and success.

1. What is church at its most basic function and essence?

2. In the Scriptures what do we see as a metric of health for local churches? How does that metric of health line up with your own metric of "success"?

3. What do we do if our definition of success is quite different than the biblical understanding of success?

4. Who—either an individual or a church—do you believe has a robust, biblically rooted and well-developed theology of failure? What could you learn from them?

5. Does our budget allow for failure?

6. Why do we do this thing called "church" in the first place? What is its purpose and intent? And what is God calling this church to become?

7. Imagine two people came to our church: one stated confidently that the church is healthy and faithful to God's mission, and the other stated confidently that it was not. Who would be right and how would we know?

8. The apostle Paul wrote letters to local congregations in the first century. If Paul wrote a letter to our congregation, what might he say?

9. If money were not a factor, how might we do ministry differently in our context?

10. How are people being formed to be more like Christ in our church?

11. Honestly, are we more focused as a church on growing hearts or on growing numbers? How would we know? Based on that answer, does anything need to change in our approach?

12. How much does fear come into play regarding leadership decisions in our church? Who or what are we most fearful of?

13. What numbers do we care about? What numbers should we care about? What numbers should we stop caring about as much? What numbers should we stop caring about altogether?

14. What stories should we be telling and celebrating together? How will we tell these stories, who will tell them, when will they be told and in what setting?

15. If Jesus appeared in the flesh at our church and looked at us and said, "What do you want me to do for you?" how would we answer?

NOTES

Introduction

[1]Paul David Tripp, *Dangerous Calling* (Wheaton, IL: Crossway, 2012), p. 86.

Chapter 1: Failure

[1]For a more thorough understanding of the dynamics of shame see Lewis Smedes, *Shame and Grace* (New York: HarperOne, 2009); and Sandra Wilson, *Released from Shame* (Downers Grove, IL: InterVarsity Press, 2002).

[2]Ken Davis, *Fire Up Your Life: Living with Nothing to Prove, Nothing to Hide, and Nothing to Lose* (Grand Rapids: Zondervan, 1995).

Chapter 2: Success

[1]Ed Stetzer, *Planting New Churches in a Postmodern Age* (Nashville: Broadman & Holman, 2003), p. 10.

[2]H. B. London and Neil B. Wiseman, *Pastors at Greater Risk* (Ventura, CA: Regal Books, 2003), p. 86.

[3]Richard A. Blackmon, "Survey of Pastors in 'The Hazards of the Ministry'" (PsyD. diss., Graduate School of Psychology, Fuller Theological Seminary, 1984).

[4]London and Wiseman, *Pastors at Greater Risk*, p. 113.

[5]Ibid., p. 62.

[6]Ibid., p. 21

[7]Ibid., p. 22.

[8]David Noble and Diane Noble, *Winning the Real Battle at Church* (Dubuque, IA: BHC Publishing, 2009), p. 17.

[9]Richard J. Krejcir, "What Is Going on with the Pastors in America?" Francis A. Schaeffer Institute of Church Leadership Development, n.d., www.intothyword.org/apps/articles/default.asp?articleid=36562.

[10]Ibid.

[11]Michael T. Wilson and Brad Hoffman, *Preventing Ministry Failure* (Downers Grove, IL: IVP Books, 2007), p. 31.

[12]London and Wiseman, *Pastors at Greater Risk*, p. 238.

[13]Krejcir, "What Is Going On with Pastors in America?"

[14]"Pastors and Internet Pornography Survey," *Leadership Journal* 22, vol. 1 (2001).

[15]Wilson and Hoffman, *Preventing Ministry Failure*, p. 31.

[16]London and Wiseman, *Pastors at Greater Risk*, p. 172.

[17]Andrew Purves, *The Crucifixion of Ministry* (Downers Grove, IL: Inter-Varsity Press, 2007), pp. 16-17.

[18]Michael Jinkins, "Great Expectations: Sobering Realities," Alban Institute, 2002, cited in Purves, *Crucifixion of Ministry*, p. 17.

[19]Tony Campolo, *The Success Fantasy* (Wheaton, IL: Victor, 1980), p. 9.

[20]Anonymous, *Embracing Obscurity* (Nashville: B & H Publishing, 2012), p. 151. See this resource for a thorough look at anonymity and obscurity in the Christian life, appropriately written by "Anonymous."

[21]Annie Dillard, *Teaching a Stone to Talk: Expeditions and Encounters* (San Francisco: Harper Perennial, 2008), pp. 36-38.

[22]Eugene Peterson, *The Contemplative Pastor: Returning to the Art of Spiritual Direction* (Grand Rapids: Eerdmans, 1993), p. 79.

[23]Henri J. M. Nouwen, *In the Name of Jesus: Reflections on Christian Leadership* (New York: Crossroad, 1989), p. 20.

[24]Wes Roberts and Glenn Marshall, *Reclaiming God's Original Intent for the Church* (Colorado Springs: NavPress, 2004), p. 13.

[25]Russ Parker, *Failure* (Nottingham, UK: Grove Books, 1987), p. 11.

[26]Steven C. Roy, *What God Thinks When We Fail* (Downers Grove, IL: IVP Books, 2011), p. 48.

[27]For a further exploration on this topic, see Wes Roberts and Glenn Marshall, "It's About Trusting God—Not Technique," in *Reclaiming God's Original Intent for the Church* (Colorado Springs: NavPress, 2004).

[28]"National Congregations Study, Cumulative Dataset (1998 and 2006–2007)," Association of Religion Data Archives, 2007, www.thearda.com/Archive/Files/Descriptions/NCSCUM.asp.

[29]"Fun Facts About American Religion," Hartford Institute for Religion Research, n.d., http://hirr.hartsem.edu/research/fastfacts/fast_facts.html.

[30]Researchers have defined megachurches as churches with more than two thousand in weekly attendance.

Chapter 3: Faithfulness

[1]Eugene H. Peterson, *Working the Angles* (Grand Rapids: Eerdmans, 1987), pp. 1-2.

[2]For a clear description of this, see Skye Jethani, *With: Reimaging the Way You Relate to God* (Nashville: Thomas Nelson, 2011).

[3]Barbara Brown Taylor, *The Preaching Life* (Cambridge, MA: Cowley, 1993), p. 16.

[4]Reggie McNeal, *Missional Renaissance* (San Francisco: Jossey-Bass, 2009), p. xvii.

[5]For a hilarious and haunting look at the powerful presence of the three Bs in ministry evaluation read Eugene Peterson's story of denominational oversight in *Under the Unpredictable Plant* (Grand Rapids: Eerdmans, 1992), pp. 77-80.

[6]Timothy Keller, *Center Church: Doing Balanced, Gospel-centered Ministry in Your City* (Grand Rapids: Zondervan, 2012), p. 97.

[7]*In the Name of Jesus* is so significant, we strongly recommend (and at times have required) Epic Fail Pastor attendees read this book before they arrive.

[8]Henri J. M. Nouwen, *In the Name of Jesus* (New York: Crossroad, 1989), p. 53.

[9]Ibid., p. 76.

[10]Ibid., p. 77.

[11]For a great exploration of redefining the metric of ministry, I recommend McNeal's *Missional Renaissance*.

[12]Keller, *Center Church*, p. 112.

[13]Dietrich Bonhoeffer, *The Cost of Discipleship* (New York: Macmillan, 1977), p. 99.

[14]Nouwen, *In the Name of Jesus*, p. 37.

Chapter 4: Shame

[1]Brené Brown shares much of her research in two of her TED and TEDx talks. TED and TEDx Conferences are hosted around the world in order to share ideas and inspire others in the areas of technology, entertainment and design. See Brené Brown, "The Power of Vulnerability," TED, *YouTube*, accessed January 1, 2013, www.youtube.com/watch?v=iCvmsMzlF7o; and "Listening to Shame," TED, *YouTube*, accessed January 1, 2013; www.youtube.com/watch?v=psN1DORYYV0.

[2]Brené Brown deserves most of the credit for the majority of the content of this chapter. I am incredibly grateful for her tireless work on such significant topics.

[3]E. Randolph Richards and Brandon J. O'Brien, *Misreading Scripture with Western Eyes: Removing Cultural Blinders to Better Understand the Bible* (Downers Grove, IL: InterVarsity Press, 2012), p. 113.

[4]Ibid., p. 119.

[5]Duane Elmer, *Cross-Cultural Connections* (Downers Grove, IL: InterVarsity Press, 2002), p. 175.

[6]Brené Brown, *Daring Greatly* (New York: Gotham, 2012), p. 44.

[7]Ibid., p. 2.

[8]Brené Brown, TEDx Houston, *YouTube*, www.youtube.com/watch?v=X4Qm9cGRub0.

[9]Ibid.

[10]Ibid.

Chapter 5: Loneliness

[1]Dan Allender, *Leading with a Limp* (Colorado Springs: WaterBrook, 2006), p. 31.

[2]Ruth Graham, phone conversation with the author, December 4, 2012.

[3]Steven C. Roy, *What God Thinks When We Fail* (Downers Grove, IL: IVP Books, 2011), p. 81.

[4]Brené Brown, *Daring Greatly* (New York: Gotham, 2012), p. 137.

[5]See Jerry Bridges, *Respectable Sins: Confronting the Sins We Tolerate* (Colorado Springs: NavPress, 2007).

[6]For a more in-depth look at masks, see Russell Willingham, *Relational Masks* (Downers Grove, IL: IVP Books, 2004).

[7]Tim Keller, "The Disobedience of Saul," sermon preached at Redeemer Presbyterian Church, New York City, January 4, 2004.

[8]Gordon, MacDonald, "The Secret-Driven Life," *Leadership Journal*, December 20, 2009, www.christianitytoday.com/le/2009/december-online-only/thesecretdrivenlife.html.

[9]John Julien, "Denial," presentation given at Metro Philly Church Planter Community, Calvary Presbyterian Church, Willow Grove, Pennsylvania, April 10, 2013.

[10]Thom S. Rainer, "Five Secrets Pastors Refuse to Tell," *Christian Post*, June 4, 2012, www.christianpost.com/news/five-secrets-pastors-refuse-

to-tell-75998/#h3IBCqq9H1BQXuV0.99.

[11]For more on the split life of pastors, see Ruth Haley Barton, *Strengthening the Soul of Your Leadership* (Downers Grove, IL: IVP Books, 2008), chap. 3.

[12]Henri J. M. Nouwen, *The Wounded Healer* (New York: Image, 1979), p. 88.

Chapter 6: Wounds

[1]Gene Edwards, *A Tale of Three Kings* (Wheaton, IL: Tyndale House, 1992), p. 19.

[2]Dan Allender, *Leading with a Limp* (Colorado Springs: WaterBrook, 2006), p. 65.

[3]For further study on the necessity of pastors dying to themselves see Andrew Purves, *The Crucifixion of Ministry* (Downers Grove, IL: InterVarsity Press, 2007).

[4]Thomas Merton, *Praying the Psalms* (Collegeville, MN: Liturgical Press, 1965), p. 27.

[5]Brian Zahnd, "God on Trial," sermon given at Word of Life Church, St. Joseph, Missouri, September 19, 2013.

[6]From C. S. Lewis, *Reflections on the Psalms* (Orlando, FL: Harcourt, 1958), p. 20.

[7]C. S. Lewis, *Reflections on the Psalms* (New York: Harcourt Brace Jovanovich, 1958), p. 23.

Chapter 7: Wilderness

[1]Ruth Haley Barton, *Strengthening the Soul of Your Leadership* (Downers Grove, IL: InterVarsity Press, 2008), p. 94.

[2]Ibid.

[3]Ray Vander Laan, "That the World May Know," *Walking with God in the Desert* (Grand Rapids: Zondervan, 2010), DVD.

[4]Ibid.

[5]Adam S. McHugh, "In Which This Is the Wilderness Life," *Sarah Bessey* (blog), March 14, 2013, http://sarahbessey.com/in-which-this-is-the-wilderness-life-guest-post-by-adam-s-mchugh.

[6]Ray Vander Laan, *Walking With God in the Desert: Seven Faith Lessons* (Grand Rapids: Zondervan 2011), DVD.

[7]I am indebted to Ray Vander Laan's research on the biblical wilderness. Many insights in this chapter come from his teaching in *Walking with God in the Desert.*

Chapter 8: Recovery

[1]*Amoral failure* is defined as the experience when a godly servant—clearly sensing the calling and leading of God—seeks wise counsel, gains affirmation, casts vision and works diligently to implement a strong plan and then experiences a ministry failure. This research did not address moral failure, recovery and restoration.

[2]There are exceptions to this generalized statement. In the interviews some pastors demonstrated the ability to move on from significant failures without experiencing any sense of loss. In each case, however, pastors had other meaningful work awaiting them.

[3]Ruth Haley Barton, *Strengthening the Soul of Your Leadership* (Downers Grove, IL: InterVarsity Press, 2008), p. 90.

[4]Elisabeth Kübler-Ross and David Kessler, *On Grief and Grieving* (New York: Scribner, 2007), p. 16.

[5]Those who write on grief recovery discuss a clear distinction between clinical depression and sadness associated with loss. This section addresses the depression associated with grieving a significant loss.

[6]Kübler-Ross and Kessler, *Grief and Grieving*, p. 21.

[7]If a pastor remains depressed for weeks or months and is not able to deal with normal daily functions, he or she may be suffering from clinical depression and needs to see a doctor.

Chapter 9: Reentry

[1]Peter Scazzero, *The Emotionally Healthy Church: A Strategy for Discipleship That Actually Changes Lives*, expanded ed. (Grand Rapids: Zondervan, 2010), p. 197.

[2]We do not suggest the goal of every situation is to lead a failed and wounded pastor back to vocational ministry. In fact, God's desires for some will be to stay out of vocational ministry permanently. Rather, the goal is to lead the pastor to health and wholeness, regardless of what that looks like vocationally.

[3]Your spouse is very much a part of your ministry and should know how to pray for and encourage you. He or she cannot be shielded from the reality of ministry life. In fact, the spouse may be just as deeply wounded as you are and just as much in need of healing. A spouse usually has no ability to interject thought or affect the outcome in a deterioration situation. Some spouses grieve in silence when their partner is attacked publicly. In some

situations the spouse is wounded more deeply than the grieving pastor. A spouse enduring the amoral failure of his or her partner will go through the grief stages as well. It is also wise for the spouse to identify a mentor or coach to help ensure his or her movement toward healing and acceptance. It is good to have someone you know is in your corner, who believes in you.

[4]Many pastors warned against bringing a spirit of criticism home. These pastors were not suggesting refraining from giving voice to these criticisms, but the critiques should be voiced in appropriate places—and home was often not the right place to do that. The proper setting for these comments (which are most likely part of the grief recovery process) is with a coach, mentor or counselor.

[5]Some suggested they mechanically sought God as a habit, while others pursued him through desperation. Just as there is no easy fix to grief recovery, there is no short-changing the importance of drawing close to God. Some may consider this counsel from recovered pastors at odds with the anger stage of grief mentioned earlier. When pastors were asked about this, they affirmed both the anger they felt over their failure and the centrality of drawing close to God. They recognized the juxtaposition, while affirming that both are necessary.

[6]If you are a coach or mentor of someone who is enduring an amoral failure, be prepared to stay relationally connected with that person for at least fourteen months after a failed ministry experience. The last thing a wounded pastor needs is to be abandoned in the midst of grief by his or her coach. Furthermore, the pastor who feels guilt for his or her inability to "snap out of it" or "get over it" should be more patient with the grieving process. When we have shared this research in various settings, many failed pastors have been able to identify that they too landed in that recovery window and found great comfort in knowing others experienced that process as well.

[7]We have two concerns regarding this seven- to fourteen-month window: (1) that some will feel guilt because they are grieving at a different pace than this window, and (2) others may give themselves permission to stop the work of processing their grief altogether. Grief recovery is a difficult, painful, time-consuming process. It is important for pastors to recognize denial, anger, depression and bargaining as it arises.

[8]None of the failed pastors Steve interviewed stayed with the group they initially connected with. That is, no wounded pastor started a church with

their nonchurched friends. God simply used those people as a source of healing for a season of the pastors' lives. Interestingly, most of these relational connections occurred within the seven- to fourteen-month window. Sometimes God, in his severe mercy and deep grace, creatively brings redemptive healing to pastors from outside of the family of God.

Chapter 10: Acceptance

[1] Richard R. Powell, *Wabi Sabi Simple: Create Beauty. Value Imperfection. Live Deeply* (Avon, MA: Adams Media, 2004).

[2] Robyn Griggs Lawrence, "Wabi-Sabi: The Art of Imperfection," *Utne Reader*, September–October 2001, www.utne.com/2001-09-01/wabi-sabi.aspx.

[3] Leonard Sweet, *Viral* (Colorado Springs: WaterBrook, 2012), p. 82.

[4] Lawrence Cunningham, *An Introduction to Catholicism* (New York: Cambridge University Press, 2009), p. 93.

[5] E. Randolph Richards and Brandon J. O'Brien, *Misreading Scripture with Western Eyes: Removing Cultural Blinders to Better Understand the Bible* (Downers Grove, IL: IVP Books, 2012), p. 143.

[6] Dan Allender, *Leading with a Limp* (Colorado Springs: WaterBrook, 2006), p. 73.

[7] C. S. Lewis, *The Voyage of the Dawn Treader,* Chronicles of Narnia 3 (New York: Collier, 1970), pp. 90-91.

[8] Margery Williams's classic children's book *The Velveteen Rabbit* talks about how pain and vulnerability are essential to the human experience.

[9] Dallas Willard, *The Divine Conspiracy* (San Francisco: HarperOne, 1998), pp. 41-42.

[10] Miroslav Volf, *Free of Charge* (Grand Rapids: Zondervan, 2005), p. 31.

[11] I first heard this phrase on a video of Robert Downey Jr. as he was introducing his friend Mel Gibson at the American Cinematheque Awards, Beverly Hills, California, October 14, 2011, www.youtube.com/watch?v=_aajuynxnTQ.

Chapter 11: Rhythms

[1] Peter Scazzero and Warren Bird, *The Emotionally Healthy Church* (Grand Rapids: Zondervan, 2003), p. 52.

[2] For more on spiritual direction, read David Benner, *Sacred Companions* (Downers Grove, IL: IVP Books, 2004).

[3] These two significant questions are found in Peter Scazzero and Warren Bird's deeply helpful book *The Emotionally Healthy Church*. Some books

are worthy of being reread with regularity. This book is one of them.

[4]The last four questions on vulnerability are from Brené Brown, *Daring Greatly* (New York: Gotham, 2012), p. 44.

[5]Brené Brown, "The Power of Vulnerability," TED, *YouTube*, accessed January 1, 2013, www.youtube.com/watch?v=iCvmsMzlF7o; and "Listening to Shame," TED, *YouTube*, accessed January 1, 2013, www.youtube.com/watch?v=psN1DORYYV0.

[6]Thomas Merton, *Praying the Psalms* (Collegeville, MN: Liturgical Press, 1965), p. 22.

[7]Peter Scazzero, *Emotionally Healthy Spirituality* (Nashville: Thomas Nelson, 2011), p. 171.

[8]Gary Harbaugh, *Pastor as Person: Maintaining Personal Integrity in the Choices and Challenges of Ministry* (Minneapolis: Augsburg Fortress, 1984), p. 47.

[9]Gary Gunderson and Larry Pray, *Leading Causes of Life: Five Fundamentals to Change the Way You Live Your Life* (Nashville: Abingdon, 2009), p. 82.

[10]Some scholars have translated the phrase *a gentle whisper* (1 Kings 19:12) as "the sound of thin silence" or "the sound of sheer silence."

Epilogue

[1]Dallas Willard, *The Divine Conspiracy* (San Francisco: HarperOne, 1998), pp. 123-25.

BIBLIOGRAPHY

Alcorn, Randy. *Money, Possessions and Eternity*. Carol Stream, IL: Tyndale House, 2003.

Allender, Dan B. *Leading with a Limp*. Colorado Springs: WaterBrook, 2006.

Anonymous. *Embracing Obscurity*. Nashville: B & H Publishing, 2012.

Balda, Janis Bragan, and Wesley D. Balda. *Handbook for Battered Leaders*. Downers Grove, IL: InterVarsity Press, 2013.

Barton, Ruth Haley. *Strengthening the Soul of Your Leadership*. Downers Grove, IL: InterVarsity Press, 2008.

Bonhoeffer, Dietrich. *The Cost of Discipleship*. New York: Macmillan, 1977.

Brown, Brené. *Daring Greatly*. New York: Gotham, 2012.

Brueggemann, Walter. *The Message of the Psalms: A Theological Commentary*. Minneapolis: Augsburg Fortress Press, 1984.

Burns, Bob, Tasha D. Chapman and Donald C. Guthrie. *Resilient Ministry: What Pastors Told Us About Surviving and Thriving*. Downers Grove, IL: InterVarsity Press, 2013.

Campolo, Tony. *The Success Fantasy*. Wheaton, IL: Victor, 1980.

Edwards, Gene. *A Tale of Three Kings*. Wheaton, IL: Tyndale House, 1992.

Elmer, Duane. *Cross-Cultural Connections*. Downers Grove, IL: InterVarsity Press, 2002.

Gibbs, Eddie. *The Journey of Ministry: Insights from a Life of Practice*. Downers Grove, IL: InterVarsity Press, 2012.

Hansen, David. *The Art of Pastoring*. Downers Grove, IL: InterVarsity Press, 2012.

Keller, Timothy. *Center Church: Doing Balanced, Gospel-Centered Ministry in Your City*. Grand Rapids: Zondervan, 2012.

Lewis, C. S. *Reflections on the Psalms*. New York: Harcourt Brace Jovanovich, 1958.

Longman, Tremper, III. *How to Read the Psalms*. Downers Grove, IL: InterVarsity Press, 1988.

McKnight, Scot. *The Jesus Creed*. Brewster, MA: Paraclete Press, 2004.

McNeal, Reggie. *Missional Renaissance*. San Francisco: Jossey-Bass, 2009.

Merton, Thomas. *Praying the Psalms*. Collegeville, MN: Liturgical Press, 1956.

Nouwen, Henri J. M. *In the Name of Jesus*. New York: Crossroad, 1989.

————. *The Wounded Healer*. New York: Image Books, 1972.

Palmer, Parker J. *Let Your Life Speak*. San Francisco: John Wiley, 2000.

Parker, Russ. *Failure*. Nottingham, UK: Grove Books, 1987.

Peterson, Eugene H. *The Pastor*. New York: HarperOne, 2011.

————. *Working the Angles*. Grand Rapids: Eerdmans, 1987.

Purves, Andrew. *The Crucifixion of Ministry*. Downers Grove, IL: InterVarsity Press, 2007.

Richards, E. Randolph, and Brandon J. O'Brien. *Misreading Scripture with Western Eyes: Removing Cultural Blinders to Better Understand the Bible*. Downers Grove, IL: InterVarsity Press, 2012.

Roberts, Wes, and Glenn Marshall. *Reclaiming God's Original Intent for the Church*. Colorado Springs: NavPress, 2004.

Roy, Steven C. *What God Thinks When We Fail*. Downers Grove, IL: InterVarsity Press, 2011.

Scazzero, Peter, and Warren Bird. *The Emotionally Healthy Church*. Grand Rapids: Zondervan, 2003.

Smith, Mandy. *Making a Mess and Meeting God*. Cincinnati: Standard, 2010.

Sweet, Leonard. *Viral*. Colorado Springs: WaterBrook, 2012.

Tripp, Paul David. *Dangerous Calling*. Wheaton, IL: Crossway, 2012.

Vander Laan, Ray. *Walking with God in the Desert*. DVD. Grand Rapids: Zondervan, 2010.

Volf, Miroslav. *Exclusion and Embrace.* Nashville: Abingdon, 1996.

————. *Free of Charge.* Grand Rapids: Zondervan, 2005.

Wangerin, Walter, Jr. *Ragman and Other Cries of Faith.* San Francisco: Harper & Row, 1984.

Willard, Dallas. *The Divine Conspiracy.* HarperOne, 1998.

Wilson, Michael Todd, and Brad Hoffman. *Preventing Ministry Failure: A Shepherd Care Guide for Pastors, Ministers and Other Caregivers.* Downers Grove, IL: InterVarsity Press, 2007.

ABOUT THE AUTHOR

 **J.R. Briggs** is founding pastor and Cultural Cultivator of The Renew Community, a Jesus community for skeptics and dreamers in Lansdale, Pennsylvania, a suburb of Philadelphia.

He is also the founder of Kairos Partnerships, an initiative that trains, equips and partners with pastors, church planters and leaders during significant kairos moments in ministry. This includes speaking, writing, coaching and consulting with churches, para-church organizations and nonprofits. Through this initiative, he serves as the director of leadership and congregation formation for The Ecclesia Network, a relational network of churches and church plants committed to remaining on mission.

He is also the creator of the Epic Fail Pastors Conference, which helps pastors embrace failure and see it as an invitation to growth and an opportunity for grace and healing.

Locally, he serves as the director of the North Penn Partnership of Churches, a unified group of churches working together for the common good of the northern region of Philadelphia in order to serve in the name of Jesus and be an ally and advocate for the community.

He is the author of and contributor to several books focusing on equipping the church and seeing followers of Jesus move into deeper levels of commitment.

J.R. and his wife, Megan, have two sons, Carter and Bennett, and live in Lansdale, Pennsylvania.

www.twitter.com/jr_briggs
www.jrbriggs.com
www.epicfailevents.com
www.kairospartnerships.org

The Epic Fail Pastors Conference was created in 2011 to provide a safe place for pastors, former pastors, church leaders and church planters to process the dangerous F-word.

That original event fueled a movement we desire to steward well. The Epic Fail Events team hosts one-, two- or three-day opportunities around the U.S. to provide hope and healing in the midst of brokenness, discouragement and failure.

These events are not intended to impress or to simply convey more information. The intent is to allow church leaders a place of refuge in order to explore the implications the gospel has on our wounds and failures, free of Christian clichés and easy answers. We listen to each other's stories, we process, we pray, we discuss, we heal, we worship, we engage in conversation, we remind each other of our hope and we participate in communion together.

Due to their uniqueness, Epic Fail Events occur only when our team is invited into a particular context. To learn more about Epic Fail Events or to bring an event to your city or region, visit www.epicfailevents.com.

IVP PRAXIS

EQUIPPING LEADERS FOR MINISTRY

"...TO EQUIP HIS PEOPLE FOR WORKS OF SERVICE,
SO THAT THE BODY OF CHRIST MAY BE BUILT UP."

EPHESIANS 4:12

God has called us to ministry. But it's not enough to have a vision for ministry if you don't have the practical skills for it. Nor is it enough to do the work of ministry if what you do is headed in the wrong direction. We need both vision *and* expertise for effective ministry. We need *praxis*.

Praxis puts theory into practice. It brings cutting-edge ministry expertise from visionary practitioners. You'll find sound biblical and theological foundations for ministry in the real world, with concrete examples for effective action and pastoral ministry. Praxis books are more than the "how to" – they're also the "why to." And because *being* is every bit as important as *doing*, Praxis attends to the inner life of the leader as well as the outer work of ministry. Feed your soul, and feed your ministry.

If you are called to ministry, you know you can't do it on your own. Let Praxis provide the companions you need to equip God's people for life in the kingdom.

www.ivpress.com/praxis